D1540960

As
American
As
Apple Pie

And 49 Other Delicious National Treasures

ELAINE CORN

Published by Prima Publishing, Roseville, California.
Member of the Crown Publishing Group, a division of Random House, Inc.

PRIMA PUBLISHING and colophon are registered trademarks of Random House, Inc., registered with the United States Patent and Trademark Office.

All products mentioned are trademarks of their respective companies.

Interior design by Melanie Haage.

Library of Congress Cataloging–in–Publication Data
Corn, Elaine.
As American as apple pie : and 49 other delicious national treasures / Elaine Corn.
p.   cm.
Includes bibliographical references and index.
ISBN 0–7615–1668–9
1. Cookery, American. I. Title.
TX715.C796   2002
641.5973–dc21   2002070364

02 03 04 05 06 07 AA 10 9 8 7 6 5 4 3 2 1
Printed in the United States of America
First Edition

Visit us online at www.primapublishing.com

★★★

For Mom and her apple pie

Contents

Acknowledgments

In this small group, some researched, some educated, some listened to babble on the phone or provided beautiful isolation on the Pacific Coast during editing. Some just chatted about food in the most stimulating and informing ways.

Thanks to Hilary Abramson, Jennifer Basye Sander, Ellie Brecher, Martha Casselman, Vivienne Corn, Darrell Corti, Dotty Griffith, Beth Hensberger, Peggy Kligman, the Muscatines, Marcie Rothman, George and Nancy Wong, and John and Shirley Wong.

As always, love and gratitude go to my husband, David SooHoo, and our son, Robert, for getting all of us through this project's baked-bean phase.

Introduction

If you want to start an argument, pose this question: What are America's most loved recipes? Chef's salad or Cobb salad? Malted or hot fudge sundae? Banana pudding or bread pudding?

To help me decide which recipes would end up in this book, I fantasized that Martians landed smack in the middle of America. Their wish was to learn to cook and eat in a manner that would make them indistinguishable from the natives. The term "recipe" was key in my choices. A peanut butter and jelly sandwich may be emblematic of the great American childhood, but it's a construction rather than a recipe. Same for S'mores.

It's clear that the 50 recipes in this book aren't enough to transform the average Martian into an American gastronome, let alone reflect which recipes deserve to enter the category "national treasure." It's important to understand the context in which we cook and eat, which is why I've included the fascinating stories of these recipes' origins. On the following pages, you'll find 50 recipes providing a broad reach into American society's primal love of food.

To build my eat-like-an-American framework, I consulted historic cookbooks and dictionaries. Many of our most-loved treasures have been around since the 1600s and are still going strong today. Pilgrims, Puritans, and subsequent boatloads of more and more immigrants set foot on North American soil, often in a relatively brutal climate. The New World was home to many delicious yet nutritious ingredients that became indispensable—corn, potatoes, turkey, maple syrup, squash and pumpkin, beans, peanuts, tomatoes, pecans, and strawberries.

It was not easy or even possible for pioneers to follow the recipes they'd brought from their homelands. Ever open-minded, the English arrivals learned from Native Americans how to make cornbread with potash, bake beans with maple, and fold native strawberries into bread. Roast turkey with cranberry sauce was ingrained then as now. The European habit of encasing just about anything in crust, along with the availability of apples and pumpkin, launched new American desserts.

To tell the stories of their origins, I researched recipes that evolved on American soil and tracked the use of ingredients. For example, one fascinating ingredient in the American repertoire is baking powder—and it *is* American. Without it we'd not know the contemporary biscuit, shortcake, quick bread, hush puppies, or cornbread.

America's favorites render a diverse profile, much like that of our population. Food habits from England became Americanized. Recipes from Italy became so Americanized that we indisputably own them. That's why, despite its origin in Naples, pizza is rightfully America's. After all, we're the folks who eat it the most *and* deliver it.

Add to the family of favorites such adoptees as guacamole, nachos, salsa, Caesar salad, chop suey, and macaroni and cheese. Over the centuries and decades, the backbone of American treasures began to include recipes that seem foreign but aren't—Eggs Benedict, cioppino, and pasta primavera. Potato salad came to America hot and in vinegar. It is to America's credit that we added Mr. Hellman's mayonnaise.

Apple pie is not American in origin, but borrowed from Europe. It resurfaced in our colonies with apples encased, like fillings in so many other pies, in an inedible crust called a "coffin." Leave it to Americans to do the right thing and rescue this doomed concept with lots of sugar, spices, and a rich short-crust pastry, making apple pie the most loved American recipe of all time.

Apple pie as a metaphor for American goodness leads to an interesting hypothesis. The phrase is probably the work of the marketing industry. At the turn of the twentieth century, the first apple marketing board, headquartered in Cortland, New York (where Cortland apples still grow), sought to polish the image of the apple and stimulate sales. The apple's reputation had been somewhat sullied. The name of Eve's forbidden fruit had become street code for "brothel." While there is no absolute proof, this reference may be at the core of the Big Apple nickname for New York City, now a sign of pride.

In any event, the campaign to restore respect to the apple was perhaps the earliest example of what modern ad execs would term "product positioning." Sloganeering spread Ben Franklin's message that "an apple a day keeps the doctor away." According to the U.S. Apple Association, Ben got his saying from an old bit of English advice: "Ate and apfel avore gwain to bed, makes the doctor beg his bread" (eat an apple before going to bed makes the doctor beg his bread). It's possible that the ultra-patriotic "American as apple pie" was introduced at this time, too. A few decades later, apples were distributed to the poor, the goodness factor in hyper mode. When and where "Mom" was inserted into the symbolic phrasing is unknown.

Real American recipes created right here in these United States sound like party food—onion dip, giant artichokes, clam chowder, baked beans, fried chicken, T-bone steak, London broil, San Francisco sourdough bread,

Buffalo chicken wings, chocolate chip cookies, strawberry shortcake, and pecan pie.

America's favorite recipes are fun to make, fun to eat, and show up at all the fun events. There is no sign that their popularity will fade anytime soon. Neither intermittent food scares, nor warnings about calorie counts, dietary cholesterol, and carbs—high or low—can keep us from our real American food. These are our favorites, and we're sticking to them.

As American as American as Apple Pie

★ Buffalo Chicken Wings ★

Not just a pub favorite, these super-spicy chicken wings show up with blue cheese dip and celery sticks at Buffalo, New York's fanciest parties, too. This combination apparently never seemed strange to folks in Buffalo, and many of them demanded the recipe from the *Buffalo News* food editor.

Years went by, but journalistic sleuthing and endless recipe tests from endless ingredient lists failed to deliver what bars all over town were making by the thousands.

Finally, a reader sent in a two-ingredient sauce. After all, how hard can a recipe be that originated in a bar?

This recipe is passed on from Janice Okun, who was food editor at the *Buffalo News* at the time of this amazing discovery.

20 to 25 chicken wings
Vegetable oil, for deep frying
¼ cup (½ stick) melted butter or
    margarine

½ to 1 bottle (2.5 ounces) Louisiana hot
    sauce, or to taste
Celery sticks
Bottled blue cheese dressing of choice

Serves 6 to 8

Cut wings in half and remove tips. Pat wings dry with paper towels.

Heat oil in a large, deep pot to 350 degrees F (use a candy thermometer). Deep fry wings, in batches (without crowding them), until golden brown, about 10 minutes. Drain well on paper towels, then transfer to large serving dish and cover.

Melt butter in a medium pot. For medium-spicy wings, add half the contents of the bottle of hot sauce. For extremely spicy wings, add the whole bottle. If you want them milder, add more butter.

Pour sauce over wings and mix well. Serve warm with celery sticks, and blue cheese dressing for dipping.

★ Oysters Rockefeller ★

The recipe for this thick anise-laced puree of green vegetables baked on fat Gulf oysters is a century-old secret credited to Jules Alciatore, owner of Antoine's restaurant in New Orleans. While trying to find something to replace snails, which were growing scarce, he came up with this dish circa 1899. The puree was rich, so he named it after the richest tycoon of the day.

Without the true recipe, desperate imitators posited spinach as the likely dominant green. When Alciatore's great-grandson, Roy Guste Jr., published *Antoine's Restaurant Cookbook* in 1979, eager readers flipped to "Huitres en Coquille a la Rockefeller." That's all they found—a title.

Ever true to the family asset, the recipe is not there. All Guste gave was one exasperating clue: The sauce is a puree made of green vegetables other than spinach.

Antoine's is perhaps the only place you can get Oysters Rockefeller made without spinach. If you've had the dish anyplace else and loved it, chances are the sauce included spinach and lots of celery leaves—just like this one.

Rock salt

2 jelly-roll pans or 4 disposable pie tins

2 dozen fresh oysters

¾ cup (1½ sticks) butter

¼ cup minced shallots

¾ cup minced celery leaves

¼ cup minced fresh Italian parsley

1 tablespoon minced fresh chervil
(or 1½ teaspoons dried)

1 bunch or bag (10 ounces) fresh
spinach, washed and wilted
(see Cooking Tips on page 4)

⅓ cup fresh bread crumbs
(see page 4)

½ teaspoon Worcestershire sauce

Salt and black pepper, to taste

Pinch of cayenne

2 tablespoons Pernod or anisette

Serves 8

Fill pans with ½-inch layer of rock salt. (If using pie tins, set them on cookie sheets.) Place pans in oven while heating it to 450 degrees F. Shuck oysters, discarding top shell and leaving each oyster with its juices in the bottom shell.

In 4 tablespoons of butter, sauté shallots, celery leaves, parsley, and chervil over medium heat until soft but not browned. Add wilted spinach, cooking and stirring another 2 minutes.

Transfer spinach mixture to a food processor or blender. Add remaining butter and the rest of the ingredients. Blend until smooth. Taste for an obvious hint of Pernod, adding a few drops more, if desired.

Top each oyster with the spinach puree. Remove the rock-salt pans from the oven. Place each oyster snugly into the hot rock salt. Return to the oven and bake until the topping is nicely golden and bubbly, about 10 minutes.

Fresh Bread Crumbs

Preheat oven to 250 degress F. Bake 4 or 5 slices of bread for 15 minutes, just long enough to slightly dry out. Run through food processor or blender until evenly crumbed. Cover tightly. May be frozen for later use.

COOKING TIPS

Wilted Spinach

- *Microwave:* Place washed, wet spinach in an 8-cup measuring glass, cover with plastic, and microwave about 2 minutes. Stir and drain in a colander, pressing out excess water.

- *Stove top:* Preheat a wok or large skillet on high heat. Add washed, wet spinach. Cook and toss, keeping the heat high, until wilted, about 2 minutes. Drain in a colander, pressing out excess water.

★ California Onion Dip ★

We are a nation of dippers, and no dip is more American than onion dip. The story goes that someone in California is believed to have concocted "California Dip" soon after the Lipton dehydrated mix's debut in 1952. The recipe made its way into a California publication, stimulating without warning a sudden surge in soup-mix sales in California. The company was smart enough to embrace the inevitable.

The original recipe was deemed too strong for mass appeal, so Lipton recipe testers adjusted the ratio of dehydrated onions to sour cream. Testing for the perfect blend was so thorough that it caused shortages of onions and sour cream near Lipton's Englewood Cliffs, New Jersey headquarters.

In tribute to the mysterious home cook who came up with the idea, Lipton called the recipe California Dip, and in 1954 launched the recipe that would create a continuous demand for sour cream. Lipton placed the recipe on the box of onion soup mix in 1958.

1 packet dry onion soup mix,
unrehydrated

2 cups sour cream

Makes 2 cups

Mix soup mix and sour cream. For crunchy dip, serve immediately. To meld flavors and rehydrate particulates, cover and chill 2 hours. Serve with potato chips or Veggie Platter (see page 10).

Onion Dip

From real onions.

  3 large yellow onions, sliced in rings
  2 tablespoons vegetable oil
  2 cups sour cream
  1 package (8 ounces) cream cheese
  1½ tablespoons Worcestershire sauce
  Few drops Tabasco
  Fresh snipped chives or fresh chopped parsley

Sweat onions slowly in oil over medium–low heat, stirring now and then, until soft, slightly shriveled, and deeply browned (about 45 minutes). Cool and chop.

Using a blender, food processor, or portable electric mixer, blend sour cream and cream cheese until smooth. Stir in onions, Worcestershire, Tabasco, and chives or parsley.

Cover tightly; chill 2 to 4 hours. Stir before serving. Serve with potato chips or Veggie Platter (see page 10).

Veggie Platter

You can't have dip without dippers. Americans, apparently too rushed to enunciate all four syllables of the English word for the edible plant kingdom, serve platters of "veggies."

Celery: Wash celery stalks, cut into 3-inch lengths.

Carrots: Peel skin, cut each carrot lengthwise into halves or quarters, then into 3-inch lengths.

Cauliflower: Separate head of cauliflower into florets, wash, then trim so each floret has a stem about 1 inch long.

Broccoli: Separate head of broccoli into florets, wash, then trim so each floret has a stem about 1 inch long.

Mushrooms: Wash mushrooms and pat dry with paper towels, then cut into ¼-inch-thick slices, discarding stems.

Jicama: Peel completely, halve lengthwise, then cut into ¼-inch-thick slices.

Green onions: Remove roots and peel off all wilted outer layers, then cut so each onion has about 1½ inches of green leaves.

Sugar snap pea: Wash and trim blossom end (the whole pod).

Green beans: Wash, string (if necessary), trim ends, then cut all to same length.

Zucchini/yellow squash: Score lengthwise with a fork for attractive pattern, halve lengthwise, then cut into ¼-inch-thick slices.

Cucumbers: Halve lengthwise and scoop out seeds, then cut into quarters to make spears.

Daikon radishes: Peel and cut as you would carrot sticks (see carrots in this list).

★ Artichokes and Dip ★

Artichokes originated in Europe, but the colossal size we favor and the way we cook and eat them are home-grown.

Europeans have grown artichokes and picked them small for centuries. Their willingness to do some time-consuming trimming and use intermediate kitchen skills to cook the thistly vegetable has enabled them to eat artichokes whole.

When Italian immigrants planted their favorite crops south of San Francisco, the Green Globe artichoke and California's climate mated for life. By 1924, the artichoke industry that still thrives in the sea-breeze town of Castroville had officially begun, this time with an American twist—jumbo dimensions.

The great size transformed the eating of an artichoke into a ritualistic use of fingers. The artichoke was not just a vegetable anymore. Its leaves became all-American dip scoops.

Mayonnaise-based dips or fillings are preferred in the West. Melted butter is the choice in the East. Most American of all is dipping artichokes in vinaigrette, ranch, blue cheese, or Thousand Island dressing straight from the bottle.

Boiled, Steamed, or Microwaved Artichokes

4 jumbo artichokes
1 lemon, for squeezing
Salt
Quick Artichoke Dip (see page 14), optional

Makes 4

Slice off stems so artichokes sit flat. Remove straggly lower leaves. Slice off entire top third of each artichoke. With scissors, cut the thorns off every remaining leaf. Rub all cut areas with lemon juice, then cook.

To boil: Add artichokes to a large pot filled with salted water and heated to a rolling boil. Drop in a few slices of fresh lemon. Return to boil, cover, reduce heat so water simmers, and cook 40 to 45 minutes.

To steam: Arrange artichokes in a steamer apparatus, sitting them on a rack over 2 to 3 inches of boiling water. Sprinkle with salt. Cover and steam 40 to 45 minutes.

To microwave: Wrap artichokes individually in plastic wrap. Set upside down on a plate in the microwave. Microwave about 15 minutes.

Place artichokes upside down on a rack to drain and cool. To eat, pick off a leaf, scrape off the interior flesh with your front upper teeth. The closer to the center, the fleshier the leaf.

Serve artichokes with an extra bowl for spent leaves, and plenty of napkins. Serve with Quick Artichoke Dip if desired.

Quick Artichoke Dips

To fill an artichoke, when artichokes cool, push apart leaves to form a bowl and expose inedible thistle. Scrape away thistle with a spoon. Fill center with dip.

- 1 cup yogurt mixed with 2 tablespoons grainy or Dijon mustard
- 1 cup mayonnaise mixed with fresh herbs, such as 1 tablespoon each minced tarragon, Italian parsley, chives, rosemary.
- 1 stick melted butter with juice of 1 lemon, plus 2 tablespoons fresh minced Italian parsley.
- Marinated artichoke hearts, with juices, from 6-ounce jar, or can pureed with 2 cups mayonnaise.

West Coast Mayo-Vinaigrette Artichokes

Prepare artichokes as described above. Spoon a tablespoon or two of mayonnaise into the center. Dribble vinaigrette over the insides of the leaves.

Artichoke Crab Meat Filling

12 ounces Dungeness or lump crab meat (enough
    to fill 4 artichoke centers)
1 rib celery, finely minced
2 tablespoons finely minced parsley
2 teaspoons tomato paste
¼ cup mayonnaise
Juice of 1 lemon
Salt and white pepper, to taste
Dash of paprika

Combine all ingredients. Fill artichoke as explained on page 14.

★ Guacamole ★

As any "avocadophile" can tell you, you need only avocados and tomatoes to replicate original guacamole. The pairing of these two fruits is ancient and unwavering. Even though the avocado was probably born in Mexico, it's reasonable to deduce that guacamole came from Peru.

Guacamole is a Nuahatl Mexican word that combines the Aztec word for avocado, *ahuacatl*, with *molli*, to mash. It is believed that the avocado was brought from Central Mexico to Peru. The ingredients for guacamole probably had their arranged marriage here, because Peru is the birthplace of the tomato.

Take an imaginary visit to the colossal market at Tenochtitlán (present day Mexico City) before its fall to Cortez in 1521 and you'll find—sold along with the roasted meats, fish, and culinary exotica demanded by the ruling Aztec class—prepared guacamole already in the form of take-out.

The first avocado tree planted in North America was in Azusa, California, just east of Los Angeles, in 1848. The Hass avocado was discovered in the late 1920s by a postman, Rudolph Hass, who found the tree in his back yard in La Habra, California. The term "guacamole" gained wide usage around 1940.

4 ripe Hass avocados
Juice of 1 or 2 limes
½ cup fresh Pico de Gallo (see page 24)
   or bottled salsa, or 1 whole ripe
   tomato, seeded and diced

Salt and black pepper, to taste
Tabasco or minced jalapeño pepper
   (optional), to taste

Makes about 3 cups

Run knife around avocado, lengthwise around the large pit. Twist the halves and pull apart. Rap knife blade into half that ends up with the pit; pull up to remove seed. Scoop out the avocado with a spoon.

Mash the avocado. If you like chunky guacamole, leave bits as you mash. If you like guacamole to be smooth, consider running the avocado through a food processor or blender. Stir in lime juice and salsa. Season with salt and black pepper. May add a few drops of Tabasco or minced jalapeño pepper.

★★★

★ Deviled Eggs ★

Food labeled "deviled" implies the possibility of ingesting the equivalent of a spicy inferno, usually in a stuffed format. The term is particularly prevalent in the American South.

The adjective was used in England and pre–New World colonies, when spicy mustard was slathered on "deviled" bones, which were re-roasted following a prime rib feast. In the colonies, the same treatment was applied to "deviled" turkey legs.

In general, a stuffing of some sort with the generous addition of cayenne, chili powder, paprika, mustard, horseradish, dried red pepper, pimento, or Tabasco (or similar bottled sauce) makes a dish "of the devil."

2 dozen hard-cooked eggs (see Cooking Tips on page 20)

4 tablespoons minced celery

4 tablespoons finely minced onion

Juice of 1 lemon

1 teaspoon Dijon or ballpark yellow mustard

4 tablespoons mayonnaise

⅛ to ¼ teaspoon cayenne pepper or hot paprika

Makes 4 dozen

Peel eggs and halve lengthwise. Scoop yolks into a mixing bowl and set emptied whites on a serving platter. Mash yolks with celery, onion, lemon juice, mustard, and mayonnaise just until mixture is combined.

Scoop mixture into egg halves. Cover and chill until ready to serve.

Just before serving, sprinkle with cayenne pepper or hot paprika.

Cooking Tips

Hard–Cooked Eggs, Perfect Every Time

Set eggs in bottom of a pot large enough to hold desired amount comfortably. Add water to cover eggs by 1 inch. Cover pot; bring to a boil over high heat. At the boil (watch for steam), remove from heat. Wait 17 minutes for residual heat to complete the cooking of the eggs.

★ Nachos ★

According to accepted history, a Mexican waiter named Ignacio "Nacho" Anaya served (but did not invent) the first batch of retail nachos in the early 1940s. While waiting on a table of women who had been shopping in Piedras Negras, Mexico, Nacho was asked to bring the group a party snack. He presented crisp-fried tortilla pieces topped with melted cheese and jalapeño slices, not an unusual border treatment for leftover tortillas. After the group ate the first platter of nachos, they ordered more, and the dish became known as the Nacho Special.

In 1977, nachos and nine innings became inseparable. The Texas Rangers baseball team had just moved to Arlington Stadium from Washington, D.C. The team finished last, but the fans didn't care. One concessionaire was selling deep-fried tortilla chips under melted Cheez Whiz (straight out of the jar) and garnished with jalapeño slices. Next season, every concession at Arlington had nachos. By the early 1980s, nachos had joined the starting food lineup at every ballpark in the country.

4 dozen tortilla chips

1 can refried pinto beans

3 cups grated cheese, such as longhorn, Cheddar, or Monterey Jack

Jalapeño slices, fresh or bottled

Serves 6

Preheat oven to 350 degrees F. Spread each tortilla chip with beans. Arrange the chips on a baking sheet. Top with cheese and jalapeños. Bake until cheese is completely melted, about 10 minutes.

★ Salsa and Chips ★

Salsa traveled from Mexico north across the Rio Grande into the Southwest United States, where restaurants would serve the egalitarian salsa and chips to all. From there the sauce migrated into our own homes.

The best salsa of all—a mixture of uncooked chopped tomatoes, onion, garlic, lime, and cilantro—is called Pico de Gallo, which means "beak of the rooster," as if a rooster had pecked the ingredients into pieces. As recently as the early 1970s, in restaurants along the Texas border, salsa arrived at the table as surely as glasses of water—and it was free. Its fresh-cut ingredients and exotic taste became irresistible on the burritos and tacos that were drifting north into America, thanks to Taco Bell, Chevy's, and El Torito. It now costs extra if the menu calls it Pico de Gallo. Homemade Pico de Gallo is still a party favorite.

Pico de Gallo

4 fresh, ripe tomatoes
1 small onion
3 cloves garlic
1 fresh jalapeño
Juice of 2 limes
½ cup minced fresh cilantro
1 teaspoon salt
Pepper, to taste

Makes 3 cups

Chop the tomatoes, and mince the onion and garlic. Remove seeds from the jalapeño; mince the pepper. Combine with remaining ingredients. Serve with chips (see page 25).

Chips

Vegetable oil
1 package corn tortillas

Makes 8 dozen

Pour 2 inches of vegetable oil into a deep skillet or deep fryer and heat to 350 degrees (use a candy thermometer). Fry fresh corn tortillas cut in eighths until the triangular pieces are lightly golden brown. Drain on paper towels and sprinkle with salt.

★ Jell-O Molds ★

To make gelatin at home, all you used to need were calves' feet, deer antlers, or sturgeon air bladders! Even in the mid–1840s, few home cooks would have gone to such trouble for this shimmery food. That's when Peter Cooper of American locomotive fame patented a gelatin powder, later produced as calves' foot gelatin by Knox in New York state. Not long after, a nearby glue–savvy carpenter named Pearle Wait fiddled with plain gelatin and additives to make it colorful and taste like fruit. His wife, May, named the bright, shiny food Jell–O.

Possibly because Wait was a carpenter and not a salesman, he got nowhere with Jell–O. He sold it for $450 to Orator Woodward, the man behind other packaged foodstuffs of the day ending in "O" (Grain-O, Rye-O). In 1925, Postum, on its way to becoming General Foods, bought Woodward's $450 investment for $67 million.

Jell–O may be convenience food, but the ability to form it into sweet and savory molds became the measure of the American housewife. Most Americans are still happy to see a Jell–O mold at Thanksgiving or Christmas, or just about any day of the year.

Salad of Gold Mold

1 package (6 ounces) Lemon Jell-O gelatin
1½ cups boiling water
1⅓ cups canned, crushed pineapple (reserve juice)
¼ cup white vinegar
1½ cups evaporated milk
1 package (12 ounces) cream cheese, cut into 1-inch cubes
2 cups peeled and diced carrots
Red-leaf lettuce (for garnish)

Serves 10

Empty contents of Jell-O package into a blender. Add boiling water and blend on low speed until dissolved. Add 1½ cups juice from canned pineapple, vinegar, and evaporated milk. With blender on, add cream cheese, cube by cube. When smooth, add carrot pieces and pineapple. Blend until carrots are grated.

Pour into an 8-cup ring mold. Chill 4 hours, or until firm.

To serve, dip the bottom of the mold into hot water. Quickly invert onto a serving platter. Decorate with red-leaf lettuce, and serve cold.

Cranberry Mold

1 package (6 ounces) raspberry Jell-O gelatin
1½ cups boiling water
1 can (16 ounces) whole cranberry sauce
1 cup cold port (or water)
½ teaspoon cinnamon
1 apple, peeled and minced
¾ cup minced celery
¾ cup chopped pecans
Green-leaf lettuce (for garnish)

Serves 10

Empty contents of Jell-O package into a large bowl. Stir in boiling water and mix 2 minutes or until completely dissolved. Stir in cranberry sauce, port, and cinnamon. Chill about 1½ hours, until slightly gelled. Stir in apple, celery, and pecans. Transfer to a 5-cup mold. Chill 4 hours, or until firm.

To serve, dip the bottom of the mold into hot water. Quickly invert onto a serving platter. Decorate with green-leaf lettuce leaves and serve cold.

⋆ Granola ⋆

The urge in the 1970s was for all things whole. Whole grains in protein combinations popular during nouveau vegetarian days eventually evolved into the yuppie chow of the '70s. They are now a supermarket mainstay.

Most likely an American rejuvenation of the Swiss mixed-grain cereal called muesli, granola had to be made at home before mainstream cereal companies added it to their product lines.

"Hippies" devised the granola we see today. They'd take a measuring cup to the bulk bins at health-food stores. After measuring dry ingredients (like the ones in this recipe) into separate bags for weighing, it was a simple matter to empty all the bags into one bowl at home. Bulk bins are now commonplace at most supermarkets.

3 cups oats

2 cups wheat flakes

1 cup rye flakes

1 cup soy flour

1 cup non-fat dry (powdered) milk

½ cup date sugar

1 cup chopped unsalted cashews

1 cup shredded coconut

½ cup vegetable oil

½ cup honey

½ cup molasses or sorghum

¼ cup brown sugar

2 tablespoons vanilla

2 tablespoons cinnamon

1 teaspoon grated nutmeg

1½ tablespoons salt

1½ cups fresh chopped Medjool dates

2 cups raisins

Makes about 2½ quarts

Preheat oven to 350 degrees F. Stir first eight ingredients in a big bowl.

In a small pot over medium heat, warm the oil, honey, molasses, and brown sugar. Remove from heat and add vanilla, cinnamon, nutmeg, salt, and dates. Pour over grains. Mix with your hands until all pieces are moistened.

Spread batches on jelly-roll pans or cookie sheets in layers no thicker than ¼ inch. Bake batches 20 to 30 minutes, stirring every 5 to 8 minutes, until evenly toasted.

Pour into a bowl. Stir in raisins and let cool. Store up to 2 months in canisters or zip-type sealable bags in the refrigerator. (At room temperature, mixture may become rancid.)

★ Biscuits ★

Undisputedly, Americans were first to leaven baked goods quickly without yeast or aeration from egg. Native Americans taught colonists that alkali ashes—literally ash from forest wood, or potash—could produce carbon dioxide that would cause dough to rise and bake into a tender bread.

It took British cookbooks decades to catch up to the chemical artistry of the New World, which is why Americans began writing their own cookbooks. *American Cookery*, published in 1796, documented that potash had been in use for decades.

Potash (or baking soda) was eventually compounded with acidic salts to produce baking powder in the 1850s. Once baking powder came to America's general stores in the mid-1860s, biscuits were rising snug in a cast-iron pan, quickly and to perfection.

Baking powder biscuits are an American specialty, made all the more tender with soft wheat flour (such as White Lily) and by acidifying the batter with sour milk or buttermilk.

2 cups all-purpose flour
2 teaspoons baking powder
½ teaspoon baking soda
1 teaspoon salt
1 tablespoon white sugar

2½ tablespoons butter plus additional
    for spreading
¾ cup buttermilk or sour milk
Flour, for dusting
Jam, for spreading

Makes about 8 biscuits

Preheat oven to 400 degrees F.

Place flour, baking powder, baking soda, salt, and sugar in a food processor. Add 2½ tablespoons butter on top. Pulse processor until mixture is evenly coarse. Transfer to a bowl. Add the buttermilk, stirring well with a fork until the dough holds together.

Scrape onto a floured board. Knead a few turns, cover lightly with a kitchen towel, and let rise 5 minutes.

Using a rolling pin, roll into a circle 1 inch thick. Cut into eight 2-inch rounds. Set rounds in a cast-iron skillet or jelly-roll pan. Bake 18 minutes, or until softly browned.

Invert biscuits onto a towel laid flat on the countertop. Serve hot with butter and jam.

★ Eggs Benedict ★

The name sounds French, but Eggs Benedict is an American improvisation. The least likely legend goes something like this: A New York drunk with a hangover entered the Waldorf Hotel's buffet line to get breakfast, where he mimicked the current rage for skyscrapers by piling an English muffin high with ham, poached egg, and Hollandaise sauce. The combination looked so impressive that the maitre d' stole the idea.

More likely, the eponym is from Mrs. LeGrand Benedict who, while lunching at Delmonico's in New York, ad-libbed an order of poached eggs over English muffins and ham topped with a thick gilded canopy of Hollandaise sauce.

Despite the recipe's saturated fat and cholesterol, health-conscious Americans continue to enjoy Eggs Benedict by the millions.

2 English muffins
Butter, for spreading
4 slices Canadian bacon or thin country
     ham

4 poached eggs (recipe follows)
Hollandaise sauce (recipe follows)
Cayenne pepper, for dusting

Makes 4

Split, toast, and butter English muffins. Top with a slice of ham, then a hot, freshly poached egg. Ladle with Hollandaise sauce, dust with the faintest sprinkling of cayenne pepper, and serve immediately.

Poached Eggs

4 eggs
¼ cup vinegar
1 tablespoon salt

Fill a 10-inch skillet with water, cover, and bring to a boil on high heat. Crack each egg into its own ramekin or cup.

Add vinegar and salt to the boiling water. Submerge the rim of each ramekin into the boiling water, and let each egg float into the water. Quickly cover the skillet, remove from heat, and let set for 4 minutes. Scoop eggs out of water with a slotted spoon.

Hollandaise Sauce

1 cup (2 sticks) butter
2 tablespoons fresh lemon juice
3 egg yolks
Pinch cayenne pepper

Serves 4

In a microwave-safe bowl, combine the butter with the lemon juice and heat for one minute on high.

Beat the yolks in a blender about 8 seconds. With the machine running, slowly pour in hot butter mixture and add the cayenne pepper. (The heat from the butter will cook the yolks.) Blend until thick and fluffy. May refrigerate up to 24 hours and reheat in the microwave, uncovered, on lowest power, stirring well every 15 seconds.

★ Breakfast Smoothie ★

Fred Waring didn't just sing with The Pennsylvanians. He liked giz-mos and gadgets, got hold of a mechanical chopping machine invented in the 1920s, and introduced the Waring "Blendor" in 1935, for which soda jerks everywhere were grateful.

The blender made it possible for the average kitchen scientist to liquefy just about anything. By 1954, Waring had sold a million of them. The blender smoothed milk, yogurt, honey, orange juice, and fruits, resulting in the luscious, fruity, thick "smoothies" we know today. Health-conscious Americans at last had a way to disguise the taste of wheat germ and brewer's yeast.

Orange-Strawberry-Banana Smoothie

1 banana, sliced
6 strawberries, washed, caps removed
Juice of 1 orange, or ½ cup commercial orange juice
2 tablespoons honey
½ cup plain lowfat yogurt

Makes 1

Combine all ingredients in a blender. Blend on a high setting until smooth and thick.

★ Cole Slaw ★

It's no coincidence that cabbage, carrots, and onion go together. In the garden, they grow simultaneously, all coming up in spring or fall. These vegetables were staples for early Dutch–Americans, and essential for their *kool sla* salad, each batch made a little differently depending on the cook. *American Cookery*, published in 1796, reflects the speed with which Americans adopted cole slaw. Author Amelia Simmons spelled the dish "slaw" before the word was listed in Webster's dictionary.

Because Fall cabbage can survive a couple of frosts, cabbage became the main cole crop destined to the root cellar along with the carrots and onions. Harvest a cabbage with its root, put it in a paper sack tied at the end, and hang it up, and your cabbage will keep up to four months. Although today associated with summer picnics, cole slaw originated as the colonists' winter salad.

Dressed with a sweet–vinegar mixture, Dutch-style, rather than with a mayonnaise–based sauce, this slaw was popularized as a side dish in New York's delicatessens.

1 large head cabbage
1 small onion, minced
1 green pepper, seeded and minced
1 carrot, peeled and shredded

½ cup plain white vinegar
¾ cup white sugar
Salt and black pepper, to taste

Serves 6

Grate the cabbage, or shred in a food processor, or slice very thin with a knife. Place in a large bowl. Add onion, green pepper, and carrot.

Combine vinegar, sugar, salt, and pepper in a small saucepan and bring to a boil, or combine them in a 1-quart glass measuring cup and microwave for 5 minutes. Pour over the cabbage and mix well. Cole slaw will compact as it is stored, covered, in the refrigerator.

★ Potato Salad ★

The sturdy potato is perhaps the most ubiquitous food on the planet. Born in Peru, it was taken to Europe post–Columbus, and came to the New World by Irish immigrants. Despite the fact that suspicious Europeans thought it was poisonous, the potato won over all doubters.

During its rise in Europe, however, the potato had a difficult time winning the love of the French. Encouragement came from Antoine Augustin Parmentier, a pharmacist who believed that a cellar of potatoes would ensure survival during a famine. One story claims that Parmentier served a dinner with potatoes in every course—in soup, cake, bread, and, yes, a potato salad. Whether Parmentier made his salad with mayonnaise isn't known.

American cookbooks of the very early 1900s already show potato salads bound with boiled vinegar dressings, sour cream, egg yolks rubbed with mustard, white sauce, and homemade mayonnaise.

America's enthusiasm for the potato salad served at home, delis, and school cafeterias seems to coincide with the introduction of commercial mayonnaise in 1912 in Richard Hellman's New York City delicatessen.

4 thin-skinned white potatoes, washed
3 ribs celery, minced
1 onion, minced
½ cup pickle relish
1 cup mayonnaise

2 teaspoons ballpark yellow mustard
2 teaspoons salt
Black pepper, to taste
3 hard-cooked eggs, chopped

Serves 6 to 8

Place unpeeled potatoes in a medium saucepan with 1 inch of water to cover. Bring to a boil, cover, then lower heat and cook potatoes 20 minutes, until a knife glides into a potato easily. Drain; cool potatoes.

While potatoes cook, combine celery and onion in a mixing bowl.

Peel potatoes; cut flesh into ½-inch cubes. Add potatoes to the mixing bowl and gently mix in the remaining ingredients. Cover, and chill before serving.

★ Caesar Salad ★

Not the product of a Roman orgy, but of Caesar Cardini, a Tijuana restaurateur who served his famous 1920s–era salad from a rolling cart bearing a wooden bowl and the salad's ingredients: coddled eggs, olive oil, garlic, fresh lemon juice, Parmesan cheese, fresh grated black peppercorns, Worcestershire sauce, and plain toasted croutons basted with olive oil—all cavorting over romaine lettuce leaves, torn not cut.

Ringside at one of Cardini's food shows was native Californian and culinary television star Julia Child, who later wrote in *From Julia Child's Kitchen:* "He didn't toss it; he scooped under the leaves to make them turn like a large wave breaking toward him, to prevent those tender shoots of green from bruising."

The flecking of anchovy in Worcestershire sauce is believed to have led to the practice of using whole anchovies. Coddled eggs gave way to raw eggs; then, in consideration of salmonella phobia, no eggs.

4 whole anchovy fillets (optional)
1½ teaspoons minced garlic
¼ cup lemon juice
Dash Tabasco
1½ tablespoons Worcestershire sauce

½ teaspoon black pepper
¾ cup olive oil
¾ cup grated Parmesan cheese
1 head romaine lettuce
1 cup plain croutons

Serves 6 to 8

Place anchovies, garlic, lemon juice, Tabasco, Worcestershire, and pepper in a blender. Blend until smooth. Stir in oil and cheese.

Discard limp outer leaves of lettuce. Wash the inner leaves, spin dry, and tear into squares.

Place lettuce in a salad bowl. Top with croutons. Toss gently with dressing, or serve dressing on the side.

★ Cobb Salad ★

Bob Cobb was the Brown Derby Restaurant's food checker, steward, buyer, cashier, and sometimes cook when the restaurant opened in Hollywood in 1926. He had partnered with owner Herbert Somborn, who had fulfilled his dream of building a restaurant shaped like a hat. Movie stars flocked to the original Brown Derby. It stayed open until all hours, serving prime beef burgers, skinless hotdogs, fresh tamales, and expensive coffee with real cream.

Before a second Brown Derby opened on Vine Street in 1929, only two items were added to the menu—a chiffon cake (later sold to General Mills) and Cobb Salad.

One day while on break, Mr. Cobb decided he wasn't in the mood for another hamburger or hotdog. In the restaurant's walk-in refrigerator, he found an avocado. He diced it and mixed it with lettuce, celery, tomatoes, a strip of bacon, and dressing. He was impressed with the 45result. A few days later, he stopped on his way to work for more ingredients. He added distinct rows of chicken, chives, hard-boiled egg, watercress, and added a chunk of Roquefort cheese in the dressing. The salad was so beautiful that, from the beginning, it was brought to the table for viewing before being tossed.

Cobb Salad

6 strips bacon
2 medium tomatoes, peeled
3 hard-boiled eggs
½ head iceberg or green-leaf lettuce
½ head romaine lettuce, halved lengthwise
½ bunch watercress, stemmed
1 small bunch chicory (curly endive)
2 chicken breasts, boiled or roasted, skinned and cubed
1 ripe avocado, cubed
½ cup crumbled imported Roquefort cheese
2 tablespoons fresh, finely snipped chives
Cobb Salad French Dressing (recipe follows)

Serves 6

Fry bacon, drain, and crumble. Halve tomatoes, squeeze out seeds, and dice. Mash eggs.

Wash and spin-dry lettuces, watercress, and chicory. Cut them finely; arrange in a wide salad bowl.

On top, arrange in strips the bacon, chicken, tomato, egg, avocado, and Roquefort. Sprinkle with chives.

Toss with ¾ cup Cobb Salad French Dressing. Serve with remaining dressing on the side.

Cobb Salad French Dressing

¼ cup water
¼ cup red wine vinegar
¼ teaspoon white sugar
1½ teaspoons fresh lemon juice
½ teaspoon salt
½ teaspoon ground black pepper
½ teaspoon Worcestershire sauce
¾ teaspoon dry mustard
1 teaspoon finely minced garlic
¾ cup vegetable oil
¼ cup olive oil

Makes about 1½ cups

Whisk, or shake in a container, all ingredients except for the oils. When blended, add the oils and whisk or shake until all elements are completely blended. Chill and shake before pouring over salad. Store well-covered in the refrigerator.

★ New England Clam Chowder ★

American chowder began no differently than most fish soups or stews from any sea in the world—from the onboard cooking of the daily catch. The word *chowder* may have originated from Breton *chaudiére* for cauldron, or English *jowter* for fish peddler. New England's most popular clam, then and now, is the big quahog. The first chowders were made with salt pork, onions, and the clam broth that resulted from the initial cooking of the quahogs themselves, making New England the rightful homeland for what America regards as the national chowder.

Potato and milk were added by the early 1800s. Starch from the potatoes added body. Considering the butterfat content of colonial farm milk, some believe that using half-and-half best approximates the consistency of those early chowders. Modern restaurants, however, have popularized clam chowder that is thick, creamy, and sometimes pasty. The West Coast, known for its dieters, favors the creamiest version of all. New England Clam Chowder remains relatively simple, thin, and milky. (Manhattan Clam Chowder is a tomato-based vegetable soup with clams.)

Clam chowder can be made with any fresh clams—cherrystone, littleneck, Manila, steamer, razor, rock, or farmed varieties. If fresh clams aren't available, you can use canned.

¼ pound salt pork or bacon, cubed

2 onions, chopped

3 russet potatoes, peeled and diced

1 bay leaf

½ teaspoon dried thyme

¼ teaspoon white pepper

2 cups clam broth (bottled, or homemade if using fresh clams)

Three cans (7 ounces each) chopped clams or 4 dozen fresh clams (see page 49)

4 cups half-and-half

1 tablespoon fresh chopped parsley

Salt, to taste

Oyster crackers

Serves 6 to 8

Fry salt pork in a large soup pot over medium–high heat until light brown. Pour off all but 2 tablespoons fat. Add onion and sauté without browning over medium heat until soft and translucent, about 5 minutes.

Add potatoes, bay leaf, thyme, white pepper, and clam broth. Bring to a gentle boil, cover, reduce heat, and simmer 15 minutes—until potatoes can be pierced easily with a knife.

Add chopped clams, half-and-half, and parsley. Taste; if chowder needs more salt, add now. Bring just to a simmer, remove from heat, and serve with oyster crackers.

Fresh Clams

2 cups water
4 dozen fresh clams, well-washed

Boil water in a large pot. Add clams, cover, and steam 4 or 5 minutes, until clams open. Remove clams from their shells over the pot to catch juices; discard any unopened clams. Coarsely chop the clams. Strain clam juice through a strainer lined with cheesecloth or a coffee filter. Reserve.

★ Gumbo ★

The multicultural culinary influences of New Orleans and Cajun country united more than 200 years ago in gumbo, a uniquely American stew that's as complex in the bowl as in its origin. The question is this: Who brought the okra, African slaves or the French?

The urban French who came to the New World by rule of the French crown are not the likely importers (although they brought the roux—a mixture of fat and flour). But another band of French pioneers (out of Southern France, as one story goes) may have become familiar with okra after it drifted to Europe, possibly from Ethiopia. In the early 1600s, these southern French pioneers immigrated to Nova Scotia and settled a colony called Acadia. By 1755, the British drove the Acadians out of Canada. Their subsequent wanderings brought them to the Mississippi Delta, where something of a reunion took place with French brethren already entrenched in New Orleans.

It's doubtful the Acadians actually brought okra with them, but it's possible they knew of its thickening prowess. Until okra got to Louisiana, Cajuns thickened stews with finely ground sassafras, called filé powder.

African slaves are most likely the ones who introduced the gummy, spear–shaped okra, which they called *gombo*, to America. In addition to its sweet taste, which blends well with tomatoes and spice, okra's gluey sap inoculated gumbo with a natural thickener as effective as filé. Everyone was happy.

Today, gumbo is made with seafood, chicken, sausage, and any sort of smoked meat. It always begins with a mahogany-colored roux.

1 cup oil

1 cup all-purpose flour

3 cups sliced okra

1 teaspoon each cayenne pepper, garlic powder, thyme, paprika, chili powder, and white pepper

4 to 6 cups warm chicken or fish stock

4 tablespoons butter

3 cups chopped onion

3 cups chopped bell pepper

3 cups chopped celery

2 tablespoons filé powder (optional)

1 can (16 ounces) crushed tomatoes

2 long links Kielbasa (smoked Polish sausage), sliced

Salt, to taste

¾ pound medium shrimp, peeled and deveined

1 pound lump crabmeat

2 pints shucked oysters

Steamed rice

Serves 6 to 8

Heat oil and flour in a cast-iron skillet, whisking, over high heat, until roux thickens and darkens to deep brown, about 20 minutes. Add okra, stirring to coat. Add spices and stock and let all ingredients heat. Remove from heat and set aside.

In a large soup pot, heat butter on medium-high. Add onion, bell pepper, and celery, and sauté about 10 minutes. Add filé (if desired for consistency) and tomatoes. Pour the roux-stock mixture from the skillet into the sautéed vegetables. Add sausage and simmer 25 minutes. Taste; add salt if needed.

Add shrimp, crabmeat, and oysters. Cook just until opaque, about 5 minutes. Serve over plain steamed rice.

⋆ Cioppino ⋆

The California fisherman's stew, popularized in the 1800s from Monterey north to San Francisco, began from the fishermen who cooked their daily catch on board.

Most similar to the Mediterranean fish stew *bouillabaise*, cioppino's influence is Italian rather than French. Many Italian immigrants who fished off San Francisco had previously fished the Ligurian Sea off the coast of Italy. In the Pacific they found wonderful ingredients to re-create *cioppin*, their shipboard stew that burbled in tomatoey broth and included a new star ingredient: Dungeness crab.

Without a true recipe, not even restaurants on San Francisco's Fisherman's Wharf make cioppino the same way their restaurant neighbors do. Family recipes and chef's preferences vary—the base can be thick or thin, spicy or bland. Besides tomatoes, fish stock, white wine, vegetables sautéed in olive oil, and maybe an indulgent pinch of saffron, fresh seafood is imperative, regardless of which seafood you choose.

1 onion, diced

1 tablespoon minced garlic

3 tablespoons olive oil

1 stalk celery, diced

⅓ teaspoon hot pepper flakes

2 teaspoons dried basil, or 1 tablespoon
fresh minced basil

½ teaspoon dried thyme

½ teaspoon dried oregano

½ teaspoon salt

1 cup dry white wine

2 cups chicken stock or water

1 can (14 ounces) tomato puree

1 tablespoon white sugar

6 cups fish (or clam) broth

2 tablespoons tomato paste

½ teaspoon saffron threads (optional)

2 Dungeness crabs, cleaned, or
12 ounces King crab legs,
hacked into 4-inch lengths

12 large shrimp, peeled and de-veined

12 mussels in shell, scrubbed

12 large scallops

12 cherrystone or Manila clams

½ pound flaky fish fillet (snapper,
flounder, cod)

½ cup fresh chopped parsley

Crusty chunks of San Francisco
Sourdough Bread (see page 65)

Serves 6 to 8

In a wide skillet, sauté onion and garlic in olive oil over medium heat until soft and clear, about 5 minutes. Increase heat; add celery, herbs, and salt, stirring. Add wine; bring to a boil, then reduce heat and simmer 10 to 15 minutes.

Strain skillet's liquid into a Dutch oven or large soup pot, pressing on vegetables before discarding them.

To the strained liquid add chicken stock, tomato puree, sugar, and fish broth. Bring to a boil; reduce heat and simmer 10 minutes. Stir in tomato paste.

Add saffron (optional), all shellfish, and fish fillet. Simmer 10 minutes.

Ladle into bowls. Garnish each serving generously with parsley. Serve with bread.

★ Pizza ★

Today Americans eat more pizza than the people of any other land, including Italy. Yet the pizza story must begin with the Etruscans in the north of Italy, who baked typical flatbread rounds. In the South, the Greeks, who occupied Sicily at that time, ritualized bread baking, often embellishing it with many ingredients. The tomato, however, wasn't one of them. It would be centuries before Columbus returned to the Old World with the tomato (the first ones were yellow), and a couple centuries more before Italians figured out that the tomato wasn't poisonous. Eventually, red tomato sauce became an Italian staple and ended up as a bread spread.

Pizza immigrated to America with Neopolitan pizza-man Gennaro Lombardi, who started baking pizza pies in the United States in 1895. By 1905, he had opened his restaurant, Lombardi's, on Spring Street in New York City. While Lombardi was starting his pizza business in America, one more tweaking had taken place. Back in Naples in 1889, a pizza-maker named Raffaele Esposito crafted a pizza in the colors of the Italian flag—using red tomatoes, white mozzarella cheese, and bright green basil leaves. He named it Pizza Margherita in honor of the queen. It was there that the classic pizza that Americans know and love really began.

In the 1940s, Americans developed a taste for new and strange toppings such as pineapple, and used their ingenuity and a bigger-is-better driving force to invent Chicago deep-dish style, a pizza so immense that eaters require a knife and fork to attack one. Now pizza is codified. New York pizza has thin crust (unless you count thick-crust Sicilian pizza, cut in rectangles and sold by the slice). New England pizza features Cheddar cheese. West Coast pizza offers vegetarian options.

Getting pizza became easier following World War II when Americans could have them delivered, and even easier with the opening of the Pizza Hut chain in 1958, followed by Tombstone in the '60s and Domino's in the '80s. Because pizza professionals put America's pizza-eating rate at about 350 slices every second, you can be sure that some-one somewhere in America is eating a pizza at this very moment. Three billion pizzas are sold at about 61,000 pizzerias across the United States each year, with Saturday night generating the highest pizza revenue.

Quick Pizza Dough

2 cups bread flour or all-purpose flour
½ cup cornmeal
1 package quick-rising granulated yeast
1 teaspoon salt
3 tablespoons olive oil
¾ cup hot water

Makes 2

Place all ingredients into a food processor. Process until dough leaves the sides of the bowl. Knead by hand a few turns. Place in an oiled microwave-safe bowl and cover with a damp towel.

Microwave on Power 1 for 5 minutes. Let set for 5 minutes. Microwave on Power 1 for 5 minutes more. Remove and let dough finish rising in a warm place, or just room temperature, until its volume doubles, approximately 30 minutes.

Topping

Cornmeal, for dusting
1 quart traditional-style bottled pasta sauce
1 package (8 ounces) thinly sliced pepperoni
1 pound fresh mozzarella cheese, thinly sliced
Freshly grated Parmesan cheese
Dried hot red pepper flakes (optional)

While pizza dough is rising, preheat oven to 500 degrees F. Dust cookie sheets with cornmeal.

Knead risen dough 1 minute. Halve; roll each piece into a thin round about 12 to 14 inches in diameter. Place rounds on cornmeal-dusted sheets. Spread with generous layer of sauce. Top with as much pepperoni and cheese as you like.

Set sheets in oven. Immediately reduce heat to 425 degrees. Bake about 15 minutes, until cheese bubbles. Remove from oven and sprinkle with Parmesan cheese. Set red pepper flakes on the table for desired sprinkling.

★ Catfish and Hush Puppies ★

Compared to such Southern lovelies as grouper, snapper, and bass, the bewhiskered channel catfish was associated with a habitat of mud and the fare of the poor. But catfish was a tradition until contemporary life nearly ruined it for good. Waters in the Mississippi Delta previously populated with decent catfish had become polluted. By the 1950s, catfish tasted like chemicals, and there was no better example of the term "trash fish."

Economic downturns for cotton and soybean farmers in the mid-1960s helped catfish bob to the top, minting money for farmers who switched to aquaculture. Today Mississippi leads in catfish production with 91,000 acres of square glistening ponds. The surprise is that today's farm-raised, grain-fed catfish tastes better than the remembered catfish of quiet streams gone by.

Catfish is so acceptable as a lowfat, high-nutrition protein that it's settled comfortably on menus in both fancy restaurants and drive-through joints, whether blackened, rubbed, sautéed, or fried. Fried catfish is Dixie's gift to the rest of the country. That one should eat it with Hush Puppies (page 63) and Cole Slaw (page 39) goes without saying.

Fried Catfish Fillets or "Nuggets"

1½ pounds catfish fillets or pieces (nuggets)
2 to 3 cups milk
1½ cups white cornmeal
1 teaspoon salt
½ teaspoon black pepper
About 1½ cups solid vegetable shortening, for deep-frying
1 lemon, cut in wedges

Serves 4

In a shallow bowl, soak catfish with milk 30 minutes. In another shallow bowl, stir cornmeal, salt, and pepper. Dredge fish in seasoned meal; let rest 10 minutes and dredge again.

In a wide cast-iron skillet, melt enough shortening to get a depth of at least ½ inch. Heat until smoking. Lay in fish and fry 5 to 7 minutes per side, until breading is golden brown. Drain on paper towels. Serve immediately with lots of lemon wedges and Hush Puppies.

Hush Puppies

Just east of the catfish's Mississippi homeland along the Florida panhandle is a Gulf town called St. Marks. Local historians attest that this is where hush puppies got their name in the early 1900s. As camp cooks fried balls of cornmeal in the hot skillets after they'd fried the fish, dogs hard on the scent of catfish barked in vain until told to hush.

¾ cup yellow cornmeal
¾ cup white cornmeal
½ cup all-purpose flour
1 teaspoon salt
1 teaspoon baking powder
½ teaspoon baking soda
½ teaspoon cayenne pepper (optional)
¾ cup buttermilk
1 egg, lightly beaten
1 medium onion, finely minced
3 cups solid vegetable shortening, for deep-frying

Makes 1½ dozen

In a large mixing bowl, stir dry ingredients together. In another bowl, whisk buttermilk with beaten egg. Pour buttermilk mixture into dry ingredients. Fold in the minced onion. Cover and refrigerate 1 hour, or until ready for use.

In a very large, wide pot, heat shortening to 375 degrees F (use a candy thermometer). Form tablespoons of batter into balls. Drop into the hot oil. Fry just until light gold. Drain on paper towels.

★ San Francisco Sourdough Bread ★

Gold miners in California and Alaska couldn't have survived the elements or hunger without their sourdough starters. Alaskan prospectors reportedly slept with their starters, keeping them warm under the covers.

Researching the cultural myth that San Francisco sourdough bread has something unique in its chemical composition, food technologists at the University of California, Davis, hit pay dirt. In tests on five of San Francisco's most famous old-starter sourdoughs, an elusive "good" bacterium was isolated. They called it *Lactobacillus sanfrancisco*. Believed to thrive only in the San Francisco area, it provides San Francisco sourdough its distinctive sourness and chewy crust.

To make sourdough in true San Francisco style takes about 1½ weeks—6 to 8 days to make a pristine, viable starter followed by up to 4 days for sponge, two slow rises, and baking. Shortcuts can produce less-sour sourdough bread in 24 hours using a quick starter, baking soda to enhance sour taste, and additional yeast to effect a decent rise.

Use Overnight Starter (page 67) or Real San Francisco-Style Starter (page 68).

One–Hour Sponge
1½ cups water
2¼ teaspoons dry yeast
2 cups bread flour

Directly in bowl of mixer (that has a dough hook), combine water, yeast, and flour with a fork until smooth. Cover; set aside for 1 hour.

Dough
One-Hour Sponge, above
2 cups starter (Overnight Starter or Real San Francisco-Style Starter)*
1 teaspoon white sugar
2 teaspoons salt
3 to 3½ cups bread flour
½ teaspoon baking soda (optional)
Cornmeal, for dusting pan
Water, for boiling

Makes 2 to 3 loaves

If you can't wait, make a preliminary loaf with dried commercial starter, such as Gold Rush brand, available at specialty groceries.

Combine raised sponge with starter of choice and sugar, salt, and 1 cup flour. Use mixer paddle attachment on low speed to blend. Mix 2 cups more flour; blend on low speed. Switch mixer to dough hook; if dough seems too wet add remaining ½ cup flour. Mix about 8 minutes on medium speed. Dough should clean sides of bowl and cling to hook.

Transfer dough to large bowl. Cover with plastic wrap and let rise in a warm place until doubled in size, about 2 to 2½ hours. Scrape onto floured board and knead a few turns. For extra sour taste, sprinkle kneading surface with baking soda and knead it into dough. Let set 10 minutes.

Portion dough into two or three pieces. Shape each piece into a smooth round. Set rounds on cookie sheet dusted with cornmeal. Cover lightly with a towel. Let rise 1 to 1½ hours.

Meanwhile, boil a teakettle full of water. Preheat oven to 375 degrees F. Have a large, shallow baking pan ready. Fill a spray bottle with water.

With a razor blade or sharp knife, gash a deep tic-tac-toe design into tops of loaves. Place loaves in oven. Set baking pan in bottom of oven; fill quickly with boiling water. Spray water onto sides of oven and tops of bread. Close door quickly. Bake 10 minutes. Spray again; bake 30 to 40 minutes more, until crust is hard and browned.

Overnight Starter

2 cups bread flour
2 cups lukewarm water
2¼ teaspoons dry yeast

Mix flour, water, and yeast in a plastic or glass container until thick. Set in a warm place overnight. Next morning, take ¼ cup starter and put it in a new container. Cover and refrigerate up to 4 months. The remaining starter may be used immediately.

Real San Francisco-Style Starter

(Requires 6 to 8 days; no sugar, no yeast)

You don't have to live in San Francisco to make sour-dough starter. However, you might name your starter L. detroit, L. newyork, or L. dallas. In 6 to 8 days, you will have bubbly living sourdough "barm" starter in its purest form—no sugar, no yeast.

5 cups tepid water
5 cups all-purpose flour or bread flour

Day 1: Mix 1 cup water and 1 cup flour in a plastic container. Leave 24 hours, uncovered, at room temperature.

Day 2: Stir in 1 cup more water and 1 cup more flour. Cover lightly with plastic wrap. Leave at room temperature two more days, stirring once a day.

Day 4: Discard half the starter. To remaining starter, stir in 1 cup more water and 1 cup more flour. Cover lightly; leave at room temperature two days, stirring once a day.

Day 6: The starter is ready if bubbles cannot be stirred down.

You'll use 2 cups of this starter to rise your first batch of bread.

What's left in the original container becomes the base for the next starter: To the remains, stir in 1 cup water and 1 cup flour. Cover and refrigerate up to 4 months.

★ Fried Chicken and Cream Gravy ★

How American is fried chicken? No European would fry like we do or eat it in a way that would elicit the description "finger-lickin.'"

Centuries before Colonel Harland Sanders started Kentucky Fried Chicken in Corbin, Kentucky, in 1956, folks in just about any American region that bred lots of chickens and lots of pigs (and in the earliest days of America, the American South had many of both) were certain to enjoy cut-up chicken fried in bacon drippings or lard.

A recipe for breaded chicken deep-fried in lard appears in the 1828 edition of *The Virginia Housewife*.

As fried chicken conquered the entire American nation, it didn't travel without controversy. Idaho, Indiana, Kentucky, Tennessee, Texas, and Hawaii have delicious fried chicken pedigrees that, for all their variations, derive from the same recipe. Small chickens or big? A batter with water, milk, buttermilk, or eggs? Cover the skillet or no? Deep-fry or pan-fry? Dredge or shake? Arguments may rage, but they share a virtuous goal—chicken that's juicy and tender on the inside, with crisp, golden brown skin on the outside. A major feat.

Fried Chicken

2 small chickens, about 3 pounds each
Gizzards and liver (optional)
¼ cup coarse salt

Coating

2½ cups all-purpose flour
2 teaspoons salt
1 teaspoon black pepper
1½ cups solid vegetable shortening
1½ cups vegetable oil

Serves 6

Cut chickens into small pieces. Breasts disproportionately larger than other pieces may be halved crosswise.

In a large bowl, place chicken, gizzards and liver (optional), salt, and enough water to submerge chicken. Soak while you prepare the rest of the ingredients.

Preheat oven to 250 degrees F. Line a baking pan with foil, and set aside. Measure flour, salt, and pepper into a paper sack.

Melt shortening in a large, deep skillet (preferably cast iron). Add oil, and heat the fats to 350 degrees F (use a candy thermometer—you will be adjusting the heat on your stove up and down throughout the cooking to maintain the proper temperature).

Remove four or five pieces of chicken from water. Dry with paper towels. Shake in the sack. Repeat shaking in small batches until all chicken pieces are coated. Reserve coating ingredients for gravy.

Cooking in batches, lower chicken into the hot oil, skin-side down. Do not allow batches to crowd the pan. Fry uncovered, turning from time to time in the oil, until golden brown on all sides, about 25 to 30 minutes. Maintain 350-degree temperature. If coating gets mushy, increase the heat.

Drain chicken on paper towels; transfer to prepared baking pan. Keep warm in oven while you fry remaining batches. Reserve cooking oil for gravy. Serve with Mashed Potatoes (see page 110) and Cream Gravy (recipe follows).

Cream Gravy

1 cup strained reserved cooking oil
1 cup seasoned flour (from the shake bag)
1 cup milk
Additional salt and black pepper, to taste

Serves 6

Heat strained oil in a skillet over medium-high heat. When hot, whisk in flour, moving the mixture constantly until flour browns, 1 to 2 minutes. Add milk, whisking, while bringing to a boil. If too thick, thin with a little water. Taste; add salt and pepper to taste. Ladle gravy over chicken and mashed potatoes.

★ Roast Turkey and Gravy ★

There's a good chance turkey was on the menu when the Pilgrims who survived their first winter at Plymouth staged a day of thanks, but it's not certain. Fowl of some sort is documented on the menu, but it could have been duck, goose, or partridge.

As times got better, Pilgrims, Puritans, and their descendants routinely held days of thanks—"thanks-givings," as they were called—and often served turkey. The bird was plentiful, fed a crowd, and was easily and completely cooked by roasting.

On October 3, 1863, a proclamation by President Lincoln reserved the last Thursday in every November for the national American holiday of Thanksgiving. The great American menu of thanks, already ritualized by borrowing heavily from two centuries of New England customs, continued to feature the great American bird.

Roast Turkey

12- to 14-pound turkey, including giblets, liver, neck, and heart
1 rib celery, washed
3 large carrots, peeled
1 large onion, peeled
¼ cup (½ stick) butter, softened
Oil
Coarse salt
White pepper

Serves 6 to 8

Preheat the oven to 350 degrees F with rack on lowest position. Cut off turkey's wrapping with scissors. Remove clamp (see Cooking Tips on page 76).

Put giblets, liver, neck, and heart in a medium pot with water to cover. Simmer, uncovered, for 2 hours, adding water if necessary. Reserve.

Cut celery, carrots, and onion into chunks; scatter over bottom of roasting pan.

Rinse turkey several times under cool running water; pat dry with paper towels. Butter and salt both cavities. Twist wing tips underneath bird; truss turkey with kitchen string. Pin flaps closed with turkey skewers or all-metal diaper pins.

Set turkey on top of vegetables in roasting pan, breast-up. Rub skin with oil, salt, and pepper. Let sit 10 minutes.

Roast 1 hour; add 2 cups water to roasting pan. Roast 1 hour more. After the second hour, check for over-browned spots; cover area(s) with foil, if necessary.

Turkey is done if the thigh's internal temperature is 175 to 180 degrees on an instant-read thermometer and juices run clear when pierced. Remove from oven; loosely cover with foil and let set 20 minutes.

Lift the turkey to a cutting board or platter for carving; reserve roasting juices for gravy (recipe follows).

To carve: With a towel over your hand, break off thigh–drumstick pieces at the natural place where the joint at the crotch cracks apart. Separate thigh and drumstick, cutting through joint. With hands, break off wings at the natural place where the joint cracks apart. Now, with a slender knife, make slices of breast meat.

Gravy

Pan juices from turkey
Liquid from the cooked giblets
Cooked giblet mixture
⅓ cup all-purpose flour
⅓ cup water
Salt and white pepper, to taste

Serves 4

Strain the roasting pan's juices into a glass bowl. Chill briefly. Spoon off fat. Remove giblets from their liquid with a slotted spoon. Chop and return to the liquid. Add de-fatted pan juices and bring to a boil.

Simmer until reduced by one-fourth. In a separate bowl, mix flour with water and add slowly, stirring to desired consistency. You may not need all the thickener. Add salt and pepper to taste. Simmer 5 minutes more.

COOKING TIPS

Turkey Clamp Removal
With a towel, pull the upside-down, U-shaped clamp toward you. With your other hand, lift each drumstick up, over, and out of the clamp. Squeeze clamp's sides in and push it away from you to free clamp.

⋆ Cornbread and Oyster Dressing ⋆

Cornbread was the only bread the country's first pioneers from England had for many seasons (see Skillet Cornbread on page 84). Their commitment to the native grain provided settlers with a default canvas for a variety of extra ingredients.

Once gardens were planted and harvested, herbs were dried and added to cornbread. Easy access to oyster beds up and down the Atlantic seaboard made it possible for coastal pioneers to combine oysters and cornbread into a delicious dish.

When used as a culinary embellishment, the South's prettier term *dressing* is preferred over the North's preference for calling the entity exactly what it is—stuffing.

Skillet Cornbread (see page 85)
2 tablespoons chopped fresh parsley
2 teaspoons dried thyme
1½ teaspoons salt
Lots of black pepper
¼ cup (½ stick) butter
2½ cups chopped celery

1 medium onion, chopped
2½ cups loose corn kernels (sold frozen
    in bags)
3 eggs
¼ cup chicken stock
1 pint jar shucked oysters or 1 dozen
    fresh oysters

Serves 8

Preheat oven to 350 degrees F. Crumble the cornbread into a large bowl. Add parsley, thyme, salt, and pepper.

Melt butter in a pan and sauté celery and onion until soft, about 10 minutes. Add to the crumbs. Stir in corn.

Beat together the eggs and chicken stock; pour over crumbs while mixing with a fork. Add oysters, juices and all, mixing them in gently.

Transfer to a buttered baking dish and cover with foil. Bake for 30 minutes. Remove foil cover and bake 30 minutes more, to brown the top.

★ Cranberry Sauce ★

*A*cidic native cranberries were the logical choice used by colonists to re-create the sweet condiment previously made in England using the equally acidic barberry. When sweetened, New England cranberries became the most popular condiments, but also provided the colonist's requirement for Vitamin C in the absence of citrus in New England's cold climate. Dating back to early colonial days, cranberry sauce was served alongside roast turkey. The addition of orange juice is a more recent variation.

1 bag (12 ounces) fresh raw cranberries

½ cup white sugar

½ cup brown sugar

½ cup orange juice

Makes 2 cups

Combine all the ingredients in a medium-sized pot. Stir until sugar is combined. Over medium heat, bring cranberries to a boil, stirring now and then. Reduce heat, simmer uncovered, until most of cranberries pop, about 20 minutes. Store, covered, in the refrigerator.

★ Chili ★

The bowl of red did not come out of the blue. Chili peppers were cooked with meat in America before Columbus arrived. An Old West legend says a range cook planted gardens with oregano, chili peppers, and wild garlic along the routes of cattle drives, which kept people in chili for a while.

Chili as a for-profit commodity was the work of San Antonio's chili "queens" of the 1800s. The queens brewed their stew by day and vended it from carts by night. The health department ended their careers in the 1930s.

It's hard to imagine today's chili cook-off mania without imaginative variations and boastful chefs, but chili-making has some rules. Rule No. 1 of the "Official Rules for Cooks" from the International Chili Society defines chili as any kind of meat, or combination of meats, cooked with chili peppers, various other spices and ingredients, except such items as beans and spaghetti, which are strictly forbidden.

In 1951 the Chili Appreciation Society was founded and set up a championship in desolate Terlingua, Texas. One of the chili cooks, Wick Fowler, rated chili intensity from one- to four-alarm, and eventually packaged his secret spice mix.

Despite its macho image, chili makes for a civil repast, as it has traditionally been eaten in parlors—that is, so-called chili parlors.

3 pounds round steak or chili grind (see
   Cooking Tips on page 83)
2 tablespoons vegetable oil
6 tablespoons chili powder
1 tablespoon dried oregano
1 tablespoon ground cumin
1 tablespoon salt
2 to 2½ tablespoons cayenne pepper
3 large cloves garlic, minced
1 tablespoon Tabasco

1½ quarts water (or enough to cover the
   meat by 1 inch)
½ cup white cornmeal or 3 tablespoons
   masa harina (optional)

Toppings

Shredded Longhorn cheese (or
   Cheddar, Colby, or Monterey Jack)
Raw diced onions or green onions
Saltines
Fresh jalapeños

Serves 4

Trim steak of fat, then cut steak into ¼-inch cubes. Heat a Dutch oven, add oil, and wait for oil to get hot. Add the meat and brown on all sides.

Pour off all but 1 or 2 tablespoons of fat. Return pan to heat, adding remaining ingredients. Scarcely simmer, cover askew (so it doesn't dry out or overflow), for 1½ hours. Remove cover and simmer 15 minutes more.

Serve chili with toppings and Skillet Cornbread (see page 85).

If a thicker chili is desired: Mix ½ cup white cornmeal or 3 tablespoons *masa harina* with enough cold water to make a thin paste. Add to the simmering stew, stirring. Cook the chili another 15 minutes.

COOKING TIPS

Chili Grind
This is a special coarse grind of round steak or chuck that is sold in mainstream grocery stores across the Southwest. If you don't see it, any butcher can run your meat purchase through a coarse setting. At home, you can make homemade chili grind by taking small quantities of your meat purchase and pulsing it in a food processor (don't grind too hard or the meat will turn to paste).

★ Skillet Cornbread ★

English arrivals in the New World were forced to use cornmeal in breads and puddings they'd previously made with oat or wheat flours. From their johnnycakes, Indian pudding, and hasty pudding, cornbread would endure throughout America the modest result of primitive chemistry.

The Indians taught early settlers that, in addition to eggs, the alkalinity of wood ash could stimulate puff in the low-gluten crumb of corn mixtures. Eventually, settlers learned that acid elements, such as buttermilk, sour milk, or molasses, when combined with the alkali, enhanced leavening.

Three centuries later, crusty cornbread is still turned out of heirloom cast-iron skillets all over America. Whether you use yellow or white cornmeal depends on your preferences. White cornmeal is ground finer and produces a creamier cornbread. Yellow cornmeal can be ground fine or coarse—as in polenta, which also dates back to colonial America—and produces a somewhat drier cornbread.

It is odd that in the South, where sugar grows, you won't find sugar in cornbread. They believe cornbread is supposed to have a sharp taste, a kind of tang. Non-Deep Southerners may appreciate a more smoothed-out taste with a small amount of sugar.

¼ cup (½ stick) butter

Dry Mixture

2 cups white or yellow cornmeal

1 teaspoon salt

½ teaspoon baking soda

½ teaspoon baking powder

1 teaspoon white sugar (optional)

Wet Mixture

1½ cups buttermilk

2 eggs

Makes 8 wedges

Preheat oven to 450 degrees F with rack on lowest position. Place butter into a 10-inch cast-iron skillet. Set the skillet in the oven.

Combine dry ingredients in a mixing bowl. In a second bowl, beat buttermilk and eggs. Pour the wet ingredients into the dry ingredients, stirring with a fork just until blended.

Using pot holders, retrieve the skillet from the oven. Swirl the melted butter so it coats the bottom and sides, then quickly pour off the butter into the batter. It will sizzle and pop. Stir the batter lightly until just blended. Immediately pour all the batter into the hot skillet.

Return skillet to oven. Bake 20 to 25 minutes. The top should be nicely browned. Let cool slightly. Cut in wedges and serve warm from the skillet.

★ Hamburger ★

In America's colonial days, minced meat mixtures with bread crumbs, cream, and spices were kneaded like sausage, flattened, rolled in crumbs, and fried. These were served as "common patties." They relate to the hamburger in form only, not in name.

The most likely ancestor of America's hamburger came from Jewish immigrants who sailed the Hamburg–Amerika line in the 1850s. To preserve meat, they salted and smoked it. When it came time to cook it, they chopped it finely and combined it with soaked breadcrumbs and onion. Once on American soil, fresh meat was made into similar patties and broiled. It was known at the time as Hamburg–style steak.

This loosely stitched legend then moves to short–order cooks, who slipped the broiled patty into a sliced bun. The hamburger was introduced at the 1904 St. Louis World's Fair.

After starring in diners and soda fountains, the hamburger catapulted to fast-food status after McDonald's applied mass production technologies in 1955. By the late 1970s, McDonald's went global, making America's original adaptation of a European beef recipe one of the most recognized symbols of America.

1 pound ground round or sirloin	½ teaspoon salt
1 egg	Freshly ground black pepper

Makes 4 hamburgers

With hands, mix meat, egg, salt, and pepper, keeping mixture somewhat loose. Separate into 4 equal patties, loosely patting into shape. For rare hamburgers, cook about 3 minutes per side using one of the following methods:

To fry: Fry over high heat in a preheated nonstick skillet until well-browned on both sides.

To grill: Place on grill rack over ash-white coals, no lid.

To broil: Place about 3 inches beneath your broiling element.

Add your choice of Fixin's (see following list) and serve with Potato Salad (see page 41), Cole Slaw (see page 39), or French Fries (see page 102).

Fixin's
Hamburger bun
Ketchup
Mustard
Mayonnaise
Sliced onion
Lettuce
Tomato
Bread-and-butter pickles

Juicy Chicken or Turkey Burgers

1½ pounds ground turkey or chicken breast
¼ cup chopped onion
½ cup bread crumbs (see page 4 for fresh
    bread crumbs)
1 egg
1 tablespoon Worchestershire sauce
½ tablespoon Dijon mustard
½ teaspoon ground black pepper
1¼ teaspoons salt

Combine all the ingredients in a bowl. Mash it
with your hands until nicely blended. Form
into 3 or 4 patties.

Fry, grill, or broil as described on page 87.

★ Meatloaf ★

Closely related to sausage (without the aging), meatloaf is an edible barometer of how our economy's faring.

Ground meats bound with bread, seasoned with exotic spices such as mace, and even moistened with actual "catsup" (as in *The Virginia Housewife* in 1824) is an American leitmotif, tracing back more than three centuries as recognizeable meatloaf.

In colonial times, the minced meats ended up baked inside a crust. Eventually, meat mixtures shed the pastry. A nearly modern meatloaf, made entirely of ground veal and baked in the familiar loaf pan, appears in *The White House Cookbook* of 1887.

Today's meatloaf is loved by more than those who admit to such common pleasures, but meatloaf has had less-than-stellar moments. During lean times, the loaf has been stretched with bread, oatmeal, left-overs, cracker crumbs, Rice Krispies, soup, tapioca, and peanut butter. Even when times were good, meatloaf's image was ruined by badly made TV dinners. A survivor, meatloaf has been elevated by modern chefs who have improved recipes with high-quality ingredients and techniques that ensure maximum moistness.

As in those early days, meatloaf remains a catchall for all manner of meat, herb, and spice. It might even taste like teriyaki or be composed of vegetarian meat substitutes yet still retain the title *meat*loaf.

Here is meatloaf with three meats that, combined, intensify flavor, moistness, and texture. You can replace any of the meats with ground turkey.

2 slices white or whole-wheat bread

½ cup milk (or water)

1 large onion, chopped

½ pound lean ground beef, such as round

½ pound ground veal

½ pound ground pork

2 eggs

½ cup chopped fresh parsley

½ cup ketchup

1½ tablespoons Worcestershire sauce

1 teaspoon salt

½ teaspoon black pepper

Serves 4 to 6

Preheat oven to 350 degrees F. In a large bowl, soak bread in the milk or water until most of the liquid is absorbed, about 3 minutes. Add remaining ingredients. Mix and mash with your hands, gently but thoroughly. You shouldn't see any chunks of bread.

Transfer to a loaf pan (no greasing necessary). Pat the meat on top. Bake 1 hour, 15 minutes.

Cool 10 minutes. Flip onto a serving platter, pouring off fat. Cut into 1-inch-thick slices. Chill uneaten portions to use in meatloaf sandwiches.

★ T-Bone Steak ★

The T-bone is actually two steaks in one. The smaller, soft buttery section on one side of the T is filet (as in mignon). The piece of meat running down the other side of the T is the boneless strip (New York, Kansas City, or shell steak).

Cowboy myth, impressive proportions, and simple cooking techniques to the American-ness of this great steak. After all, the French don't serve bone-in beef with buckaroo tendencies. By the mid-1850s, steak was already considered America's most typical main course. On ranches and cattle drives of the same era, cowboys who ate beans and biscuits all week wanted steak—a big one—by the weekend. The thicker the T-bone, the better it cooks. Where cuts of chuck, arm, brisket, and rump require long, slow cooking, a T-bone can be cooked the American way—fast.

The popularity of the T-bone has fallen behind the boneless strip, filet, prime rib, and top sirloin. Meat with bones spoils faster than boneless cuts, so restaurants must sell T-bones quickly. On home grills, however, the T-bone remains the king of carnivores, as it was back on the trails.

Grilled T-Bone Steak

2 to 4 T-bone steaks, 1½ inches thick
Salt and black pepper

Serves 2 to 4

Bring steaks to room temperature. Prepare a grill with white hot coals. Just be-fore cooking, generously salt and pepper the steaks.

Grill about 7 minutes per side (10 minutes per total inch of thickness). When it's reached desired doneness, remove with tongs to a serving plate. Wait 5 minutes before slicing.

Panfried T-Bone Steak

2 T-bone steaks, at least 1¼ inches thick
Salt and black pepper
1 cup red wine or vermouth

Serves 2

Bring steaks to room temperature. Heat a large cast-iron skillet over high heat. Just before cooking, generously salt and pepper the steaks.

Add steaks to the skillet, setting them in opposite directions, like shoes. Reduce heat to medium-high. Fry steaks 5 to 7 minutes per side for medium-rare.

When desired doneness, remove steaks from skillet to a serving plate. Turn heat to high. Add wine or vermouth to the pan drippings. Scrape up bits stuck to the bottom of the pan as liquid boils. Boil until slightly reduced, 1 to 2 minutes. Pour sauce over steak.

★ London Broil ★

London Broil isn't from London. And it's not the name of a cut of beef. It's the name of a recipe that propagated through word of mouth until the cut and the recipe fused as one.

The term entered the American vernacular after a recipe called "London Broil" first appeared in print in the early 1930s.

The original recipe specified flank steak, which is from under the cow's belly just behind the ribs. The steak was marinated, then broiled or grilled, and carved specifically across the grain into thin slices.

Other cuts such as beef tip, round steak, or beef chuck shoulder steak have since been used. Since the inception of the London Broil recipe, however, London Broil has been practically synonymous with flank steak.

1 beef (2 pounds) flank steak	1 cup soy sauce
1 tablespoon fresh minced garlic	1 tablespoon Worcestershire sauce
1 medium onion, minced	2 tablespoons brown sugar (or honey)
1 cup dry red or white wine (or flat beer)	Fresh ground black pepper

Serves 6

Lightly score the meat. Combine remaining ingredients in a lidded container jar and shake well. Pour over meat. Marinate 2 hours at room temperature, or up to 24 hours, covered, in the refrigerator.

Bring meat to room temperature before grilling. Lift meat out of marinade. Strain marinade into a small pot and simmer 5 minutes.

Grill steak over hot coals, or broil, about 4 minutes per side. Baste well with the warm marinade. Meat should be medium-rare.

Cut in very thin slices across the grain. Serve with choice of French Fries (see page 102), Mashed Potatoes (see page 110), Potato Salad (see page 41), or Cole Slaw (see page 39).

★ Barbecue ★

Americans claim to have invented many things, but cooking raw animal flesh over an open fire isn't one of them. However, meat prepared in such a manner in America can be regionalized into various and distinct areas. Regardless of location, it's all called *barbecue*, a term in use in America since the 1600s.

Beginning in colonial North Carolina, pork and vinegar formed a perfect union over flame. Sauces evolved to include mustard, sugar, tomato, hot peppers, garlic, ginger, and vegetables such as celery. In the cattle-driving West, beef replaced pork. Native Hawaiians have pit-cooked Kalua pig for centuries.

The tradition of guys standing around in the backyard grilling meat slathered with sauce contributed to an American mania replete with cook-offs and proud pontificators. Now, excellent store-bought sauces make barbecue one of the nation's easiest, quickest meals.

4 to 5 pounds pork spareribs (about 2 big slabs)

1 onion, chopped

1 green pepper or hot banana pepper, seeded and chopped

1 long rib celery, diced

¼ cup white vinegar

Juice of 1 lemon

2 cans (8 ounces each) tomato sauce

1 cup ketchup

2 tablespoons brown sugar

2 teaspoons salt

1 tablespoon Worcestershire sauce

¼ teaspoon ground ginger

¼ teaspoon ground cloves

½ teaspoon ground black pepper

Few shots Tabasco

Serves 6 to 8

Preheat oven to 450 degrees F. Place ribs in a large shallow baking dish. Place in oven 20 minutes, until meat releases about 2 tablespoons fat. Remove ribs from oven. Reduce heat to 350 degrees.

Pour off fat into a large saucepan, leaving ribs in baking dish. Over medium-high heat, sauté onion, green pepper, and celery in hot fat until onion is lightly browned. Add remaining ingredients, bring to a simmer; simmer 15 minutes, stirring.

Pour sauce over ribs. Bake 2 to 3 hours, basting every 30 minutes.

★ Chop Suey ★

Chop suey is most decidedly a Cantonese stir-fry. What makes it American is the form it took in this country and the name assigned to the form.

In village Cantonese dialect, chop suey translates to "mixed miscellaneous." A familiar legend says gold miners, weary from traveling from the mother lode back to San Francisco, entered a Chinese restaurant and asked the chef to make something. Placed before them was a dish known to any Chinese cook—a humble stir-fry of mixed miscellaneous ingredients—in this case pork strips, bean sprouts, celery, and onions—all seasoned with oyster sauce and served over rice.

"What is this?" the miners asked. "Tsap tsui," was the cook's storied answer. His limited English had named a category of Chinese cooking, not the name of an actual dish.

The miners loved it, and the misfiring of language prevailed for this particular mix of ingredients. To please Americans, chop suey appeared for nearly a century on menus of Chinese-American restaurants, even the fine ones, decked out with snow peas and bamboo shoots, or made alternately with chicken. Before long, Chun King canned it and Woolworth's was serving it at its lunch counter.

12 ounces pork butt (Boston-style shoulder), in thin strips (may use chicken)
1 tablespoon soy sauce
⅛ teaspoon white pepper
2 teaspoons, plus 2 tablespoons cornstarch
2 tablespoons oil
1 onion, sliced
1 cup diagonally sliced celery
½ cup drained bamboo shoots

½ cup fresh sliced mushrooms
½ cup drained water chestnuts
¼ cup chicken broth
2 cups fresh bean sprouts
½ pound fresh snow peas, strings and caps removed
2 tablespoons oyster sauce
Salt, to taste
Rice

Serves 4

Marinate pork in soy sauce, white pepper, and 2 teaspoons cornstarch 10 minutes.

Heat a wok, add oil, wait for oil to smoke, then add marinated pork. Stir-fry until lightly browned, about 45 seconds.

Add onion, celery, bamboo shoots, mushrooms, water chestnuts, and chicken broth. Stir, bring to a simmer, cover, and steam about 2 minutes.

Open lid, add bean sprouts and snow peas, tossing. Cover and cook 1 minute more.

Uncover, add oyster sauce and salt and white pepper, to taste.

Mix remaining 2 tablespoons cornstarch with 3 tablespoons water and add mixture quickly. Boil, uncovered, about 20 seconds, until thickened. Serve over rice.

★ French Fries ★

While minister to France, Thomas Jefferson was served *pommes frites*— potatoes "frenched" with a knife into long lengths and deep-fried. Good American that he was, he seemed to develop a helpless passion for them and did what any great host would do. He served them at Monticello, explaining to guests that these were potatoes "in the French manner." By 1824, his descendent Mary Randolph had included a recipe for French fries in her cookbook *The Virginia Housewife*.

Belgium is still upset with France over this; the Belgians believe that the French fry is theirs. The saga of possession continued until World War I, when American GIs in France ate fries and dubbed them "French fries."

In the glory days before mass-production, French fries were rinsed in water before being deep-fried twice in some form of animal fat, yielding fries crisp on the outside, flaky on the inside, and savory all around.

Some believe that McDonald's did more for the French fry than it did for the hamburger. During its first 10 years under Ray Kroc, when French fries accounted for barely 5 percent of all potatoes sold, McDonald's spent more than $3 million to perfect its French fries, including field technology that produced Russet potatoes of exactly the same size.

Today, 25 percent of all potatoes sold in the United States end up fried "in the French manner." The fast-food secret is to fry twice, first at 250 degrees F, then at 360 degrees.

4 russet potatoes

4 cups solid vegetable shortening

Salt, to taste

Serves 4

Peel potatoes and cut into French-fry lengths. Place in a bowl and cover with water. Let soak while you heat the shortening.

In a large pot or deep-fryer, heat the shortening to 250 degrees (use a candy thermometer). Fry potatoes in batches, and without crowding, about 3 minutes. Drain on paper towels.

When ready to serve, heat same shortening to 360 degrees. Fry potatoes in batches, and without crowding, until golden brown, about 8 minutes. Drain again on paper towels; sprinkle with salt while hot.

★ Baked Beans ★

If you like baked beans, thank the devout Puritans. What put pots of beans on so many Boston and New England tables was the requirement of rest on the Sabbath. In order not to cook on Sunday, beans were cooked for hours throughout Saturday evening. When the Sabbath came, the beans were reheated, relieving home cooks of work.

Long before colonists arrived in the New World, dried beans sustained Native Americans. In transferring their knowledge of indigenous beans, the English embraced the Native Americans' method for baking dried beans. Heirloom beans such as Yellow Eye, Jacob's Cattle, or Soldier beans were mixed with maple syrup and sometimes venison, fish, or corn. When it became available, molasses replaced maple syrup, and salt pork became the primary seasoning meat. Today it's up to the cook which sweetener to use.

1½ pounds Great Northern or navy
    beans, sorted and soaked overnight
    or by Quick Soak method
    (see below)

1 onion, minced
1½ tablespoons dry mustard
1 cup molasses
½ pound salt pork, diced

Serves 10

Quick Soak: Rinse beans under cool water and place them in a Dutch oven with enough water to cover. Bring quickly to a boil, uncovered; reduce heat and simmer 2 minutes. Remove from heat, cover, and let stand 1 hour.

Drain soaking liquid. Place drained beans in a Dutch oven. Add enough fresh water to cover beans by 1 inch. Simmer uncovered until tender, 45 minutes to 1 hour.

Preheat oven to 300 degrees F. Drain beans over a bowl, reserving beans' cooking liquid. In a lidded heavy casserole, combine the drained beans, onion, mustard, molasses, and salt pork. Add enough reserved cooking liquid to submerge beans, then stir.

Bake, covered, at 300 degrees for 3½ hours. Add more bean liquid if beans dry out. Remove cover. Finish baking, uncovered, 30 minutes more.

★ Macaroni and Cheese ★

The contents of Kraft's blue box might trace its American ancestry to Thomas Jefferson. The third president endured several bouts of near-bankruptcy. Could his recipe for boiled macaroni baked with grated cheese have been the prudent rib-sticker in a mansion otherwise full of French wine?

One thing is certain: While America's macaroni and cheese started off as a naive stab at something remotely Italian, it remains a true American favorite you'd have a hard time finding in Italy.

Through the centuries, Americans have prepared macaroni and cheese Jeffersonian-style (with grated cheese), as well as with layers of white sauce and cheese. The Depression made a star out of elbow macaroni and Kraft's yellow "American cheese."

1 pound elbow macaroni

¼ cup (½ stick) butter, plus some for
    greasing

4 tablespoons all-purpose flour

2½ cups milk

½ teaspoon salt

White pepper, to taste

1 pound grated Cheddar or longhorn
    cheese

Pinch cayenne pepper

Serves 4 to 6

Cook macaroni according to package directions. Drain and reserve. Preheat oven to 400 degrees F. Butter a 2-quart baking dish.

In a medium saucepan over medium-high heat, melt butter. Add flour, whisking well, until a bubbling paste is formed, about 2 minutes.

Add milk slowly, whisking out lumps. Simmer and stir until thick, about 4 minutes. Remove from heat. Add salt, pepper, and cheese, blending until cheese melts. Add cayenne.

Mix cheese sauce gently with cooked macaroni. Transfer to the baking dish. Bake, uncovered, for 30 minutes.

★ Pasta Primavera ★

Pasta Primavera was invented by an Italian restaurateur vacationing in Canada.

In 1975, Sirio Maccioni, owner of Le Cirque in Manhattan, attended a conference in Canada with the food press. The Nova Scotia seafood was delicious, but rich. Deciding to make a light dish for the group, Maccioni's shopping produced spring vegetables and, of course, spaghetti.

He turned out something like fettuccine Alfredo, but with a lighter cream sauce to go with the vegetables. The group loved it and demanded the name of the dish.

"Spaghetti Primavera" didn't have the right ring. But the alliterative Pasta Primavera (translation: springtime pasta) had a nice sound.

Within a few months, the *New York Times* wrote about Maccioni's Pasta Primavera, printed his recipe as Maccioni could best remember it, and a craze was born. Despite its Italian pedigree, you're unlikely to find Pasta Primavera in Italy.

1 pound spaghetti

1 cup sliced zucchini

1 cup sliced broccoli florets

1½ cups snow peas, ends trimmed

1 cup frozen petite peas

6 stalks asparagus, trimmed and cut in
    1-inch lengths

10 mushrooms, sliced

2 tablespoons olive oil

2 tomatoes, coarsely chopped

¼ cup fresh minced parsley

1 teaspoon salt

Ground black pepper, to taste

2 teaspoons minced garlic

⅓ cup pine nuts

½ cup finely grated Parmesan cheese

5 tablespoons butter

1 cup heavy cream

⅓ cup fresh chopped basil leaves

Serves 6

Cook spaghetti according to package directions. Drain.

In a large saucepan, steam zucchini, broccoli, snow peas, petite peas, asparagus, and mushrooms in 1/4 cup water, covered, until tender, about 5 minutes. Drain vegetables in a colander.

Return saucepan to stove. Add 1 tablespoon olive oil and heat until smoking. Add tomatoes, parsley, salt, and pepper, and sauté about 3 minutes; keep warm.

Meanwhile, in a large skillet, heat remaining tablespoon olive oil over high heat. Add garlic and pine nuts, tossing in the pan about 20 seconds. Add steamed vegetables and bring to a simmer. Add cooked spaghetti, Parmesan, butter, cream, and basil. Toss well in the skillet until butter melts.

Transfer pasta to a serving platter. Pour tomato mixture on top. Serve warm.

★ Mashed Potatoes ★

When Americans say meat and potatoes, they probably mean meat and mashed potatoes. Since the 1700s, America's earliest cookbooks recommended potatoes with roast beef, a "steake," a chop, or fricassee. A century earlier, a common nutrient–rich side dish was potatoes mashed with boiled turnip or parsnip, available all winter from the root cellar. For variety, the mixture might take in some browned onion, perhaps a precursor to today's rage for garlic mashed potatoes.

Back in Europe around the turn of the nineteenth century, the French were finding potatoes so malleable that they'd perform in just about any way a chef wanted. In particular, the Duchess–style features the potato—boiled; pureed with butter, salt, pepper, and maybe some nutmeg; and ready for the pastry bag—piped in designs around the border of the plate.

It is this mixture, as seen in an American recipe published as early as the 1820s calling for potatoes mashed with butter and milk, that probably influenced our reliable current style for mashed potatoes.

So important are mashed potatoes to the American home cook that it's a rare household that doesn't have a tool for the single purpose of mashing potatoes.

3 or 4 large russet potatoes, peeled and
cut in chunks
3 tablespoons butter

½ cup milk (or cream)
½ teaspoon salt
White or ground black pepper, to taste

Serves 4

Bring potatoes to a boil in salted water to cover, uncovered. At the boil, cover, reduce heat, and cook potatoes 12 minutes, until a knife tip can easily glide through potatoes.

Drain water out of the pot, leaving potatoes in the pot to dry somewhat. Mash with butter, milk, salt, and pepper until desired consistency, or whip with portable electric beaters. Serve hot.

Garlic Mashed Potatoes

1 entire head garlic
Mashed Potatoes (see page 110)

Chop off the entire root end of the garlic, exposing ends of cloves. Wrap in foil and set in a small ovenproof dish. Bake at 400 degrees F for 1 hour.

Squeeze the soft garlic paste into the prepared Mashed Potato recipe, stirring to blend. Serve hot.

⋆ Apple Pie ⋆

For centuries apple pie was made without mention of mom or any other wholesome symbol. Apples came to America from Europe, where apple pie had been served even before the French chef Taillevent baked one gussied up with figs and raisins for the king in the 1400s.

Early sojourners to the New World were proud of their pies, but not pies for dessert. More common was to fill top and bottom pastry (called paste) with pigeon, meats, mincemeat mixtures, carrots, or cod. The apple pie served at that time might not have even had the benefit of sugar, just fruit stewed in its own juices.

As colonial apple orchards matured in America and sugar supplies improved, the sweetened Old World pie was revived, this time with scores of American apple varieties. Many pies included cinnamon or cloves and a final swish of rosewater or lemon brandy. The crust remained unsweetened for nearly a century.

This is my book, so I'm using my own mom's glorious apple pie recipe. It dates to the 1930s, which means my grandmother, who lived in the shore area of New Jersey in sight of the Statue of Liberty, made it before Mom did.

The recipe is titled "Washington Apple Pie." It is unknown whether the reference is to the state or George. Most likely, it refers to the State of Washington, possibly engaged in a consumer campaign to encourage home cooks to buy and use apples. The filling uses Dole pineapple juice.

The technique that prepares the apples for the pie, to me, is the reason for its perfection. Whoever developed this recipe taught me that no great apple pie can possibly be made using raw apples. I was happy to see precooking the apples validated as early as 1833. Author Lydia Maria Child, in *The American Frugal Housewife*, scolded cooks who cut apples directly onto the crust rather than briefly pre-cooking them so seasonings would mix in better.

My mother expended much effort on this pie, as do I today. Not impressed with the looks of pies topped with bulky cover crusts, my grandmother and mother always took the extra time to weave an artistic lattice crust.

Double Golden Pie Crust (see page 115)
10 to 12 medium apples (Granny Smith, Pippin, or Gravenstein)
1 cup sugar
1 cup unsweetened pineapple juice
2 teaspoons cinnamon

2 tablespoons butter
1½ teaspoons vanilla
1 tablespoon cornstarch dissolved in ¼ cup water
1 egg yolk mixed with 3 tablespoons milk

Makes 1 pie

Prepare crust. Roll out bottom crust, line pie plate, and refrigerate until needed.

Preheat oven to 450 degrees F. Peel and core apples; cut into eighths. In a large pot, bring sugar and pineapple juice to a boil until sugar dissolves. Add apples; lower heat and simmer until apples are barely tender but not soft, about 8 minutes. Stir occasionally, taking care not to break apple pieces. With a slotted spoon or strainer, remove apples to a cookie sheet to cool, then transfer to the chilled pastry.

To the juices in the pot, add cinnamon, butter, and vanilla. Bring to a boil. Add the cornstarch mixture. Boil while stirring constantly until thick, about 30 seconds. Remove from heat and spoon sauce over apples.

Roll out remaining crust, cut into strips ¾-inch wide and weave an attractive lattice top. Around the circumference, tuck the overhang of dough underneath itself, then crimp. Brush with egg yolk/milk wash.

Place pie on a cookie sheet. Bake for 20 minutes. Reduce heat to 350 degrees; bake 35 minutes more, until crust is golden brown and apple filling is bubbling.

Cool completely on a wire rack before slicing. Store in the refrigerator wrapped well in foil or plastic wrap.

Golden Pie Crust

Single crust	Double crust
1¼ cups all-purpose flour	2 cups all-purpose flour
¼ teaspoon salt	½ teaspoon salt
½ teaspoon sugar	1 teaspoon sugar
8 tablespoons very cold butter, in pats	11 tablespoons very cold butter, in pats
1 tablespoon very cold solid shortening	3 tablespoons very cold solid shortening
3 tablespoons ice water	5 tablespoons ice water

Place flour, salt, and sugar in a food processor. Top with butter and shortening. Pulse until consistency of coarse meal. With machine running, pour in ice water. Process just until dough forms a ball. Halve the dough and flatten into two disks with rolling pin. Wrap separately in plastic and chill until ready to use.

⋆ Pumpkin Pie ⋆

So vital was the native "pompkin" to American colonists that a delayed shipment of molasses in 1705 caused an entire city in Connecticut to postpone Thanksgiving until there was enough molasses for pumpkin pie.

In everyday life, even plain boiled pumpkin provided high-quality nutrition to wave after wave of new immigrants. Europeans applied their tradition of encasing fillings in pastry to mashed or pureed pumpkin meat. As molasses, sugar, and eggs increased in availability, and shipping companies brought spices from the opposite side of the world, savory pumpkin pie evolved into sweet, puffy, and custardy, and finally mated with all or a choice of nutmeg, cinnamon, allspice, and clove. It's still the easiest pie of all to make.

Golden Pie Crust, single 10-inch
  (see page 115)
1½ cups fresh pumpkin puree, drained
  (or 1-pound can solid-pack
  pumpkin)
1 cup heavy cream, plus ½ cup additional cream for whipped-cream
  decoration

½ cup milk
4 beaten eggs
1 cup light brown sugar
1 teaspoon cinnamon
¼ teaspoon ground cloves
½ teaspoon nutmeg

Makes 1 pie

Preheat oven to 400 degrees F. Set a rack in the lowest notch. Roll out crust
and line pie plate.

Combine all filling ingredients in a big mixing bowl using a whisk.

Pour into the pie shell. Crimp crust.

Set the pie on a cookie sheet. Bake for 10 minutes. Reduce heat to 350 degrees and bake 1 hour more. Check halfway through; rotate pie if necessary
for even browning.

Pie is done if a table knife inserted 2 inches from edge comes out clean.
Serve warm or cold decorated with whipped cream.

★ Lemon Meringue Pie ★

Acrobatic egg cookery and perfect timing make Lemon Meringue Pie the mark of a superb cook. With its English–style lemon curd and fancy French meringue on top, how is it American?

The most likely ancestor is the European lemon tart, common since the 1600s. By the early 1800s, recipes were being published in America for a curd–type lemon pudding. It very closely resembled the filling used in modern lemon–meringue pies.

Southern cooks most likely completed the look of the lemon meringue pie we'd recognize today. A Virginia recipe printed during the 1820s shows a kind of bread custard topped with meringue and browned under a salamander (the broiler in old stoves). But farther South and toward the end of the 1800s, cooks would plop sweet meringue on top of banana pudding, then bake it fast at high heat until the tips browned.

It's possible that cooks disliked the bleak, plain surface of a lemon tart and decided that the lofty meringue treatment would make a great topping.

Lemon Pie

Golden Pie Crust, single (see page 115)
3 to 4 lemons
1½ cups white sugar
½ cup cornstarch
Pinch salt
1⅔ cups water
6 egg yolks
3 tablespoons butter
Meringue (see page 120)

Makes 1 pie

Preheat oven to 425 degrees F. Roll out crust and line pie plate. Crimp, line with foil, and bake for 15 minutes. Remove foil and bake 10 minutes more. Remove from oven and cool.

Grate enough zest off lemons for a total of 2 teaspoons finely minced; reserve. Juice the lemons until you have ⅔ cup lemon juice.

Pour lemon juice into a saucepan. Add sugar, cornstarch, salt, and water. In a separate bowl, beat egg yolks until smooth. Add yolks to lemon mixture along with butter, stirring to blend. Cook over medium heat, stirring constantly, until mixture thickens and starts to boil. Boil 1 minute, stirring. Remove from heat; add zest. Pour lemon curd into the baked pie crust.

Spread meringue on pie's edges first, sealing. Fill center with big tufts of meringue, making high swirls. Bake about 10 minutes, until tips are lightly browned. Cool to room temperature before cutting. Cuts best with a knife dipped in hot water, then wiped dry.

Meringue

6 egg whites
¼ teaspoon cream of tartar
¾ cup white sugar
½ teaspoon pure vanilla extract

Makes enough topping for 1 pie

Preheat oven to 350 degrees F. Beat egg whites and cream of tartar to stiff peaks. Continuing to beat, add sugar slowly, then vanilla, until glossy and very stiff.

★ Pecan Pie ★

Low, swampy soil from East Texas and points eastward is the natural habitat of America's native pecan trees. It was nothing unusual for Southern cooks to combine pecans and another local crop—sugar—in candies, particularly after the French improved confectionary in New Orleans. How pecans and sugar jumped together into a pie remains somewhat of a mystery, though one indisputably owned by the South.

Molasses pie or brown sugar pie, two of America's easiest and sweetest creations, were definitely on the table by the early 1800s. With sugar and pecans commonplace, it wasn't much of a stretch to place them together in a setting where they'd be comfortable.

It's even easier to understand the early 1900s introduction of high-fructose corn syrup, or "invert" sugars. Karo (pronounced kay-roe) Corn Syrup became pecan pie's greatest defense against crystallization, a disaster for those cooking sugar. Karo fostered the baking of pecan pies, becoming as much a staple in the recipe as the pecans.

Golden Pie Crust, single (see page 115)
2 large eggs
1 cup light or dark corn syrup
½ cup white sugar
3 tablespoons all-purpose flour
½ teaspoon salt

Pinch cinnamon
1 teaspoon pure vanilla extract
2 cups pecan halves
¼ cup melted butter
Whipped cream

Makes 1 pie

Preheat oven to 300 degrees F. Roll out crust and line pie plate. In a large mixing bowl, whisk eggs until completely blended. Whisk in corn syrup, sugar, flour, salt, cinnamon, and vanilla until smooth. Stir in pecans and melted butter. Pour into unbaked pie crust. Crimp crust. Place cookie sheet under pie plate.

Bake for 1 hour. A knife inserted near the center should come out clean.

Cool on a wire rack. Cut with a knife dipped in hot water, then wiped dry. Serve with a big dollop of whipped cream topping on each slice.

★ New York Cheesecake ★

Printed evidence of cakes baked with dry ricotta cheese dates to the 1470s in Italy. The cheesecake Americans love comes from New York's immigrant communities at the end of the 1800s. The main ingredients were cream cheese, sugar, and eggs. America's first cream cheese came from a farmer in upstate New York. The stimulus recipe that precipitated our cheesecake mania quite possibly came right off a package of Philadelphia Cream Cheese introduced in 1880 and later sold to Kraft.

Retail-wise, cheesecake is a product of theater-district Jewish delicatessens. Whether it was Reuben's delicatessen, where claims of cheesecake date to 1929, or Lindy's citrusy version, which shuns graham crust in favor of short pastry with egg yolk, remains a gratuitous argument. America's devotion to cheesecake favors Lindy's style, known as New York Cheesecake everywhere except in New York. It cuts as though it's dry, but coats the mouth with a smoothness every cheesecake lover longs for.

Crust

Seeds from 2-inch piece of vanilla bean

1 cup all-purpose flour

¼ cup white sugar

1 teaspoon grated lemon zest

2 egg yolks

1 stick cold unsalted butter, cut in bits

¼ teaspoon salt

Filling

2½ pounds cream cheese, at room temperature

1¾ cups white sugar

3 tablespoons all-purpose flour

1½ teaspoons grated orange zest

1½ teaspoons grated lemon zest

½ teaspoon pure vanilla extract

5 whole eggs

2 egg yolks

½ cup sour cream

¼ cup heavy cream

Topping (optional)

2 cups sour cream

½ cup powdered sugar

Makes 1 cheesecake

Preheat oven to 400 degrees F. Combine vanilla seeds, flour, sugar, and zest in a bowl. Add egg yolk, butter, and salt. Knead briefly, until mixture forms a dough. Flatten into a disk, wrap in plastic, and chill at least 1 hour.

Press two-thirds of the dough into a ⅛-inch thick layer on the bottom only of a 9-inch springform pan. Bake bottom crust 10 to 12 minutes, until golden. Butter the pan's side-piece, attach it to the bottom, then press the rest of the dough ⅛-inch thick onto the side, sealing it to the bottom crust. Set aside.

Increase oven temperature to 550 degrees, with the rack in the center.

Beat cream cheese, sugar, flour, zests, and vanilla until smooth, preferably with paddle attachment of electric mixer. Gently beat in the eggs one at a time, beating only until blended, stopping the mixer after each addition. Stir in sour cream and heavy cream.

Pour filling into prepared crust. Bake 12 minutes. Lower heat to 200 degrees and bake 1 hour more.

Turn off oven and cool cheesecake in the oven with the door ajar. Remove from oven. When completely cool, run a small knife around the edge to loosen, then remove side of the pan. Wrap cake in plastic; chill overnight before slicing.

Sour cream topping (optional): Beat sour cream with powdered sugar. Spread over cheesecake, hiding any cracks.

★ Peach Cobbler ★

A cousin to the deep-dish pie but a direct descendant of the American biscuit, cobbler began its rise in the 1860s with the help of a magical, new ingredient—baking powder.

Before 1860, cobbler had a top and bottom crust that did not contain baking powder. More like pie crust, the top crust might be broken and stirred into the warm filling and served with plain cream. This type of cobbler was considered a member of the fruit pudding family.

With baking powder commercially available, dough for cobbler and biscuits intermarried. Biscuit dough already had proven foolproof with baking powder. Somehow home cooks transferred dough from its usual place in a cast-iron pan to rise on top of sweetened fruit.

Biscuit-topped cobbler is just one type. Baking powder proved so effective an ingredient that cobbler batter could rise from beneath the fruit as well, as this old Texas/Georgia recipe proves.

8 to 10 medium fresh peaches, peeled
(see Cooking Tips on page 128)
¾ cup brown sugar
1½ teaspoons cinnamon
1 tablespoon cornstarch

½ cup (1 stick) butter
1 cup all-purpose flour
1 cup white sugar
1 tablespoon baking powder
¾ cup milk

Serves 6

Slice peaches and remove pits. Gently mix them with brown sugar, cinnamon, and cornstarch. Meanwhile, allow stick of butter to melt in a 9-inch by 13-inch baking dish in the oven as you preheat it to 350 degrees F.

Stir together flour, sugar, baking powder, and milk until the mixture is the consistency of pancake batter.

Remove pan with melted butter from the oven. Immediately pour in batter. Do not mix.

Spoon peaches over batter. Return to oven and bake 45 minutes, or until the crust rises over the fruit and browns well.

Scoop out servings while warm. Serve with cream or vanilla ice cream.

Blackberry Cobbler

For blackberry cobbler, use 6 cups fresh or frozen blackberries (drained) instead of peaches.

Cooking Tips

To Peel Peaches

Place fresh peaches in a large bowl. Bring a teakettle full of water to a rolling boil. Pour the hot water over the peaches and let stand a minute or two. Skins should loosen. Pierce skin with a paring knife and peel off.

★ Banana Pudding ★

When trains began overland shipping of bananas imported from South America, they began their journey into America at New Orleans. They traveled a route up the Mississippi River that took the bananas to Fulton, Kentucky. Here, the bananas were iced before heading just about anyplace else in the United States.

Originally made with leftover sponge cake a la trifle, Banana Pudding topped with brown-tipped tufts of lush meringue is now commonly layered with Nabisco Nilla Wafers.

1 cup white sugar
½ cup all-purpose flour
4 cups milk
6 egg yolks
1 tablespoon vanilla
3 tablespoons unsalted butter
1½ cups cream
1 box (7.5 ounces) vanilla wafers
Bourbon, for sprinkling
6 bananas, thinly sliced
Meringue (see page 131), optional

Serves 12

Whisk sugar, flour, and milk in a heavy saucepan until free of lumps. Cook over medium heat, stirring constantly with a wooden spatula, just to a boil.

Combine some of the hot pudding with the egg yolks; pour the yolks back into the main pudding mixture, whisking well. Return to heat for 1 minute, stirring. Add vanilla and butter. Cover with plastic wrap and chill.

Whip cream to stiff peaks. Fold into cold pudding.

Line a 10-cup baking dish with half the vanilla wafers. Dribble with bourbon. Pour one-third of the pudding over the wafers, then half the bananas. Add another layer of wafers, sprinkle with bourbon, then the next third of pudding and remaining bananas. End with a final layer of pudding and tufts of meringue, if desired.

Meringue

6 egg whites
¼ teaspoon cream of tartar
½ teaspoon pure vanilla extract
¾ cup white sugar

Preheat oven to 350 degrees F. Beat the egg whites and cream of tartar to stiff peaks. Gradually add the ⅔ cup sugar, then vanilla, beating again until stiff and glossy.

Pipe or swirl meringue over the pudding. Place 10 to 15 minutes until meringue tips are browned.

★ Strawberry Shortcake ★

Shortcake is the rich cousin of the biscuit or scone—yellower from egg, sweeter from sugar, and dense from cream. Like many older American classics, shortcake is low-tech, requiring a couple of bowls, a fork, and some cake pans.

The 1833 edition of *The American Frugal Housewife* recommends making shortcake to serve with tea to use up sour milk or buttermilk—just as is done today.

American Indians had eaten small, native wild strawberries for centuries and used them ceremonially. The Iroquois cultivated them. They also crushed the berries before mixing them with cornmeal to produce strawberry bread.

The colonists may have roused the American imperative that bigger is better. Once sugar and quick leavening became available, it wasn't much of a leap from strawberries in cornbread to strawberries on top of sweet biscuit—now an emblem of the American summer.

2 cups all-purpose flour
½ cup, plus 2 tablespoons white sugar
¼ teaspoon salt
1 tablespoon baking powder
½ cup (1 stick) unsalted butter, in bits
    and chilled
1 egg, beaten

⅔ cup half-and-half
2 cups heavy cream
2 teaspoons pure vanilla extract
2 pints red ripe strawberries, washed
    and hulled
1 tablespoon lemon juice

Serves 6

Preheat oven to 425 degrees F. Generously grease a cookie sheet. Pulse flour, ¼ cup sugar, salt, and baking powder in food processor. Set butter pieces on top; pulse a few times until mixture is mealy. Transfer to a mixing bowl.

In another bowl, whisk egg and half-and-half. Stir into dry ingredients to form a sticky ball. Scrape dough onto a floured surface. Knead a few times until the dough holds together.

Roll dough about 1 inch thick. Cut into 6 3½-inch rounds and set the rounds on the cookie sheet. Bake for 12 to 15 minutes, until golden. Cool slightly; remove from sheet and cool on wire rack.

Whip cream, 2 tablespoons sugar, and vanilla to nearly stiff peaks. Chill.

Crush one-third of the strawberries with remaining ¼ cup sugar and lemon juice. Slice remaining berries, then mix with the crushed berries.

Split cooled shortcakes horizontally. Spoon strawberries and a dollop of whipped cream onto the bottoms. Add tops, more strawberries, and more whipped cream.

★ Hot Fudge Sundae ★

Before we can discuss the hot fudge sundae, we must first discuss ice cream and the sundae itself.

Because of references to Marco Polo returning from the Orient to Europe with a recipe for a frozen milk concoction, it is undisputed that ice cream was made in France by the early 1700s. It was kept cold with snow and ice.

Enter Thomas Jefferson on assignment to France. He encountered ice cream in the so-called French style which involved a cooked custard base. He recreated ice cream back home at Monticello in a hand-operated sorbetière, using local cream and eggs and vanilla pods brought from France.

Even the hardship of preserving ice cut in winter through summer in icehouses insulated with straw could not separate Americans from their ice cream. Dolley Madison, wife of President James Madison, who was the era's "hostess with the mostess" as well as Jefferson's host during his bachelorhood, never let a warm summer day stop her from serving ice cream. It is believed she was the first to add strawberries, creating America's first strawberry ice cream.

American ingenuity (or impatience) eventually shortened the ice cream–making process. The custard stage was dashed and replaced by a rich ice cream made Philadelphia-style by simply agitating chilled cream, sugar, and vanilla.

With the recipe for ice cream entrenched, creativity swirled over its uses. In Evanston, Illinois, during the 1890s, strict Christian observance of the Sabbath discouraged such pleasures as drinking soda on Sundays. Ice cream with syrup on top—a Sunday—became an approved substitute Sabbath pleasure—until church overseers deemed that appropriating the name of the Sabbath day for an indulgent treat was heretical. The spelling of the word was then altered to "sundae."

Hot fudge on ice cream was a daring teaming of elements of opposing temperatures. C. C. Brown claims to have been the first to ladle hot fudge sauce on cold vanilla ice cream, at his downtown Los Angeles restaurant in 1906. In 1929, C. C. Brown's moved to Hollywood Boulevard, where movie stars lined up for French vanilla ice cream topped with roasted chopped almonds and real whipped cream, all in a silver goblet, with hot fudge sauce presented in a pitcher on the side.

2 scoops vanilla ice cream
(recipe follows)
2 teaspoons chopped roasted almonds
Hot Fudge Sauce (recipe follows)

Whipped cream (see Strawberry
Shortcake recipe on page 133)
Maraschino cherry (optional)

Makes 1 sundae

Place two scoops of ice cream in a goblet. Top with almonds, Hot Fudge Sauce, whipped cream, and a cherry, if desired. Serve immediately.

Vanilla Ice Cream

The ultimate easy, rich ice cream, the uncooked Philadelphia-style is American simplicity at its best.

2 eggs
1 cup white sugar
2 cups cream
1½ cups milk
2½ teaspoons vanilla

Makes about 1¼ quarts

Beat eggs and sugar until fluffy and sugar dissolves. Whisk in cream, milk, and vanilla. Transfer to electric ice cream maker and freeze according to manufacturer instructions.

Hot Fudge Sauce

1 cup cream
¼ cup dark or light corn syrup
6 ounces semisweet chocolate, finely chopped
4 tablespoons unsalted butter, cut in small pieces
½ teaspoon vanilla

Makes 2½ cups

In a small saucepan, bring the cream and corn syrup to a boil. Remove from heat; stir in chocolate until it melts completely. Return to very low heat; stir in butter until just melted. Remove from heat and add vanilla. Pour over ice cream.

Store covered in refrigerator up to 2 months. May reheat in microwave for 20 seconds, uncovered, stirring well.

★ Chocolate Chip Cookies ★

The Toll House Chocolate Chip Cookie was the creation of Ruth Wakefield, owner of the Toll House Inn in Whitman, Massachusetts. In 1930, Mrs. Wakefield published a cookbook of her inn's recipes. In it was the first printed recipe for chocolate chip cookies. Her cookies were small, crunchy, didn't have nuts, and were baked at a rather high 375 degrees F.

They did not contain the ingredient we know today as chocolate chips, which hadn't been invented then. To make chips, Mrs. Wakefield chopped up Nestle's semisweet chocolate bars. With an opportunity akin to the one Lipton faced when a consumer used onion soup mix to make dip (see California Onion Dip on page 7), Nestle's happily joined the chocolate chip cookie rage. In 1939, Nestle's produced chocolate morsels, and home cooks no longer had to chop chocolate.

But the Toll House cookie, as popular as it was for decades, would be improved by its imitators. Like many American favorites, the chocolate chip cookie underwent a transformation. Thanks to Debbie Fields, owner of Mrs. Fields' cookies with outlets in 57 countries, the chocolate chip cookie is bigger, fleshier, and with fat chocolate chunks instead of mere morsels.

1 cup (2 sticks) butter (or margarine)
1½ cups white sugar
1 cup brown sugar
2 eggs
1 tablespoon vanilla

3 cups all-purpose flour
1½ teaspoons baking soda
1½ teaspoons salt
3 cups semisweet chocolate chips

Makes 2½ dozen big cookies

Preheat oven to 350 degrees F. In large bowl blend the butter, sugars, eggs, and vanilla with an electric mixer until very creamy, about 2 minutes. In another bowl, combine flour, baking soda, and salt. Add flour in three helpings to the butter mixture, mixing each time on low speed just until blended. Stir in chips.

Scoop portions of dough with large spoon onto ungreased cookie sheets (don't use black bakeware). Leave 2 inches between cookies.

Bake for 12 to 15 minutes. Cookies will seem limp and unset; leave on cookie sheet 5 minutes after removal from oven. Cool cookies on wire rack.

Bibliography

Anderson, Jean. *The American Century Cookbook: The Most Popular Recipes of the 20th Century.* New York: Clarkson N. Potter, Inc., 1997.

Appelbaum, Diana Karter. *Thanksgiving: An American Holiday, An American History.* New York: Facts on File Publications, 1984.

Better Homes and Gardens. *Heritage Cook Book.* Des Moines, IA: Meredith Corporation, 1975.

The Brown Derby Cookbook. Garden City, NY: Doubleday & Company, Inc., 1949.

Child, Lydia Maria. *The American Frugal Housewife: Dedicated to Those Who Are Not Ashamed of Economy.* Boston, MA: Carter & Hendee, 1833. Facsimile, Bedford, MA: Applewood Books, 1990.

Corn, Elaine. "Nachos," *Louisville Courier-Journal,* March 18, 1983.

_____. "Go Bananas," *Louisville Courier-Journal Sunday Magazine,* May 9, 1982.

_____. "On the T–Bone Trail," *Sacramento Bee Sunday Magazine,* January 8, 1989.

Egerton, John. *Southern Food.* Chapel Hill, NC: University of North Carolina Press, 1993.

First Ladies White House Cookbook, Bicentennial Edition. New York: Parents Magazine Press, 1975.

FitzGibbon, Theodora. *The Food of the Western World.* New York: Quadrangle/The New York Times Book Co., 1976.

Flexner, Marion. *Out of Kentucky Kitchens.* New York: American Legacy Press, 1949.

Food Editors and Writers Association. *Food Editors Hometown Favorites, Two Volumes in One.* Edited by Barbara Gibbs Ostmann and Jane Baker. Maplewood, NJ: Weathervane, 1986.

Fussell, Betty. *The Story of Corn.* New York: Alfred A. Knopf, 1992.

Griffith, Dotty. *Celebrating Barbecue: The Ultimate Guide to America's 4 Regional Styles of 'Cue.* New York: Simon & Schuster, 2002.

_____. "Nachos Pitched First to '77 Ranger Fans," *Dallas Morning News,* October 13, 1993.

Hiatt, Judith. *Cabbage, Cures to Cuisine.* Happy Camp, CA: Naturegraph Publishers, 1989.

Hopley, Claire. *New England Cooking: Seasons & Celebrations.* Lee, MA: Berkshire House Publishers, 2001.

Mariani, John F. *The Dictionary of American Food and Drink.* New York: Ticknor & Fields. 1983.

Nathan, Joan. *Jewish Cooking in America.* New York: Alfred Knopf, 1994.

Randolph, Mary. *The Virginia House-wife.* Washington: Printed by Davis and Force, 1824. Facsimile, *The Virginia House-wife, With Historical Notes and Commentaries by Karen Hess.* Columbia, SC: University of South Carolina Press, 1984.

Royal Cookbook. New York: Royal Baking Powder Co., Inc., 1929.

Simmons, Amelia. *American Cookery.* Hartford, CT: Hudson & Goodwin, 1796. Facsimile, *The First American Cookbook.* New York: Dover Publications, 1984.

Simon, Frederick J. *The Steaklover's Companion.* New York: HarperCollins, 1997.

Sparks, Elizabeth Hedgecock (Beth Tartan). *North Carolina and Old Salem Cookery.* Kingsport, TN: Kingsport Press, Inc., 1955.

Trager, James. *The Food Chronology: A Food Lover's Compendium of Events and Anecdotes, from Prehistory to the Present.* New York: Henry Holt and Company, 1995.

Wyman, Carolyn. *Jell-O: A Biography. The History and Mystery of America's Most Famous Dessert.* New York: Harcourt, Inc., 2001.

Zieman, Hugo and Mrs. F. L. Gillette. *The White House Cookbook: A Comprehensive Cyclopedia of Information for the Home.* New York: The Saalfield Publishing Company, 1887. Reprint, *The Original White House Cookbook.* Old Greenwich, CT: Devin Adair Company, 1983.

Index